Cambridge Elements

Elements in Phonetics
edited by
David Deterding
Universiti Brunei Darussalam

SOCIAL FACTORS AND L2 PHONETICS AND PHONOLOGY

Jette G. Hansen Edwards
The Chinese University of Hong Kong

Shaftesbury Road, Cambridge CB2 8EA, United Kingdom

One Liberty Plaza, 20th Floor, New York, NY 10006, USA

477 Williamstown Road, Port Melbourne, VIC 3207, Australia

314–321, 3rd Floor, Plot 3, Splendor Forum, Jasola District Centre, New Delhi – 110025, India

103 Penang Road, #05–06/07, Visioncrest Commercial, Singapore 238467

Cambridge University Press is part of Cambridge University Press & Assessment, a department of the University of Cambridge.

We share the University's mission to contribute to society through the pursuit of education, learning and research at the highest international levels of excellence.

www.cambridge.org
Information on this title: www.cambridge.org/9781009468169

DOI: 10.1017/9781108943062

When citing this work, please include a reference to the DOI 10.1017/9781108943062

First published 2024

A catalogue record for this publication is available from the British Library.

ISBN 978-1-009-46816-9 Hardback
ISBN 978-1-108-93202-8 Paperback
ISSN 2634-1689 (online)
ISSN 2634-1670 (print)

Social Factors and L2 Phonetics and Phonology

Elements in Phonetics

DOI: 10.1017/9781108943062
First published online: February 2024

Jette G. Hansen Edwards
The Chinese University of Hong Kong

Author for correspondence: Jette G. Hansen Edwards, jhansen@cuhk.edu.hk

Abstract: This Element provides readers with a detailed overview of the social factors that affect second language (L2) phonology acquisition and use. Through a state-of-the art synthesis of the relevant literature, this Element addresses the following questions:

- What do we mean by social factors?
- Which social factors have been investigated in research on L2 phonological acquisition and use?
- How and why do social factors affect L2 phonological acquisition (production and perception) and use?
- What are the implications of the social factor findings for teaching L2 pronunciation?

The Element answers these questions through a synthesis of key findings in research on social factors and L2 phonology. Conclusions and implications for teaching, as well as key readings and references, follow the research synthesis.

Keywords: social factors, L2 phonetics, L2 phonology, sociolinguistics, gender

ISBNs: 9781009468169 (HB), 9781108932028 (PB), 9781108943062 (OC)
ISSNs: 2634-1689 (online), 2634-1670 (print)

Contents

1 Introduction

This section presents and defines the major concepts of the Element, including phonetics, phonology, and social factors. In addition, it provides an overview of the focus of the Element, including the populations and contexts from which the research synthesized in it is drawn.

1.1 Phonetics and Phonology Defined

It is important to first define what we mean by *phonetics* and *phonology*. Phonetics is the study of speech sounds. In this Element, phonetics refers to the individual segments of speech – the consonant and vowel sounds – that learners acquire and use in their second language (L2) or second dialect. The sounds /d/ (*den*) and /ð/ (*then*) as examples are consonant speech sounds. Slant brackets are used to denote the underlying representation of each sound – /d/ is a voiced alveolar stop and /ð/ is a voiced dental or interdental fricative, also called a voiced TH. These are individual phonemes of a language. Square brackets are used to denote how a sound is actually physically realized in a language/variety or by a speaker. The voiced TH /ð/, for example, may be variably realized as [d] (*that* as *dat*) or [ð] (*that* as *that*) in some varieties of English. The realization of the dental fricative as the stop [d] is referred to as DH-stopping.

The study of phonology concerns the patterns of individual speech sounds at the level of the syllable as well as stress and intonation. An area of phonology that is often studied in research on social factors is voice onset time (VOT), a feature of stop consonants, particularly when they are in initial position in a word and/or syllable. Voice onset time refers to the duration of time between the release of a stop consonant and the onset of vocal fold vibration for the following vowel. It differs for voiced and voiceless consonants as well as across languages. For example, VOT in English for word initial voiceless stops is longer than VOT in Spanish, and therefore a speaker with Spanish as their first language (L1) may have a shorter VOT in L2 English than an L1 speaker of English. This will be one aspect of this speaker's L2 accent.

Throughout this Element, reference is made to Wells' (1982) lexical sets, a set of keywords developed by John C. Wells to categorize vowel inventories of English. While developed primarily in reference to General American English (GAmE), a standard variety of American English, and Received Pronunciation (RP), a standard variety of British English (BrE), the lexical sets have been widely used in research on varieties of English. Each keyword represents one vowel sound found in either GAmE or RP or both. As an example, TRAP refers to the vowel /æ/, a low front vowel found in both GAmE and RP in words such as *tap*, *hand*, and *back*. Whenever a word appears in full capitalization, as in TRAP, GOOSE, FOOT, *HAPPY*, and *LETTER*, these words represent lexical sets. A full list of Wells' lexical sets with vowels and example words can be found in the Appendix. Readers are encouraged to refer to the Appendix when lexical sets are referenced.

1.2 Defining Social Factors

The Element addresses several key questions:

- What do we mean by social factors?
- Which social factors have been investigated in research on L2 phonological acquisition and use?
- How and why do social factors affect L2 phonological acquisition (production and perception) and use?
- What are the implications of these findings for teaching L2 pronunciation?

To answer the first two questions – *What do we mean by social factors?* And *Which social factors have been investigated in research on L2 phonological acquisition and use?* – Social factors can be defined as factors that are external to the learner and/or part of the language learning environment. In the study of the acquisition and use of L2 phonetics and phonology, a range of social factors have been examined, including the factors examined in this Element: L2 attitudes (Section 2), social and peer group networks (Section 3), L2 contact and exposure (Section 4), study abroad (Section 5), gender (Section 6), and identity and ethnic group affiliation (Section 7). These factors are often considered individual difference factors, as they may help explain individual differences or differential outcomes of L2 acquisition and use. Individual differences encompass factors that are considered internal to the language learner, such as personality traits (extroversion and introversion), language learning aptitude, motivation, age, and anxiety, factors that help us understand differences in L2 learning outcomes. As such, social factors can be considered a subset of individual difference factors, the factors that focus on the impact of the social context(s) and the learner's relationship with the social context, on L2 acquisition and use. Each of the factors covered in the Element will be defined in more detail in the following sections.

1.3 Social Factors and the Social Context

To answer the third question – *How and why do social factors affect L2 phonological acquisition (production and perception) and use?* – the study of social factors can help us understand how the learner's interaction with the social environment, and the different linguistic features in their environment(s) result in the use of specific phonetic and phonological features within and across social contexts. In other words, the study of the impact of social factors on L2 acquisition and use helps us explain differential L2 learning outcomes through an examination of the speech sounds to which the learner is exposed, and targets for acquisition and use. The sounds that learners target for acquisition and use may be influenced by the speech norms in their L1 and L2 communities and gendered speech norms in these communities. Learners may also retain L1 features and target L2 features to construct a viable L1 and/or L2 identity. Exposure to a range of L2 features different from what is taught in the L2 classroom through the mass media, study abroad opportunities, and the social and ethnic peer social networks learners may develop will influence what learners target for acquisition and use.

Learners are exposed to multiple varieties of a given language outside the language classroom and, in some cases, inside the language classroom, due to ethnic, regional, or social differences that may exist in a particular language context. Therefore, learners may be exposed to a range of accents, not only the standard language variety. The L2 model and linguistic features that are taught in classrooms may not be the learner's actual target for acquisition and use. As I have argued previously (Hansen Edwards, 2008, p. 251):

> learners are active agents in their language use, language choices, and targets for acquisition. That is, they are not passive recipients of the target language, and variation in production is typically systematic and may be due, in part, to social marking due to gender, identity, accommodation to the interactant, and the linguistic environment, etc. As a result, differences between the target language and the language of the learner may not necessarily be errors but may be evidence of users targeting a particular variety that is not necessarily the standard or marking their identity by using a certain variant in a specific situation with interactants.

Equally, a learner may choose to resist or avoid using features of the L2 that conflict with a desired or established L1/L2 identity and/or social group membership(s).

A number of points are important to the discussion in this Element: (1) the learner's awareness of how particular L2 speech features and norms are used within and across the different speech communities as well as L1 and L2 use contexts to which they have access or wish to belong; (2) the learner's ability to perceive the phonetic and phonological features in use in different social groups or contexts, which may be enabled or restricted by social factors; and (3) the learner's actual ability to modify their pronunciation towards the features they wish to target and/or mark a particular identity or social group membership.

An important focus in the discussion of social factors is resistance to or avoidance in using specific features of the L2, and that L2 use which differs from standard norms may not be incomplete learning of the L2 but may instead reflect the learner's acquisition and use of particular speech norms based on social factors such as gender, identity, and social and peer networks. Success in acquiring an L2 is typically measured by how well the learner approximates a standard language norm, the educational model in most language classrooms. When a learner uses L2 pronunciation features (or other linguistic features) that differ from standard norms, the assumption is often that they have incomplete acquisition of the L2. As an example, an L2 learner of English pronouncing *that* as *dat* with DH-stopping, the realization of the voiced TH as the voiced alveolar stop [d], may be viewed as having failed to acquire the voiced TH. While this is one potential explanation, several others are possible as well: (1) the learner has acquired [ð] and may use it interchangeably with the voiced stop depending on the social situation and interactant(s); (2) the learner is able to produce the voiced TH but may avoid or resist using it in most social situations; and (3) the learner is not able to produce the voiced TH and avoids targeting it for acquisition and use. As these different scenarios suggest, the use of linguistic features that differ from standard language norms may not be errors or signify lack of acquisition, but may instead be active choices by the learner to target or avoid usage of particular features, possibly due to social factors such as gender, identity, and social and peer networks. A final important point to note is that linguistic features – for example, using [d] or [ð] in *that* in English – may not have the same social meaning in different dialects, regions, or social groups. Therefore, it is necessary to study the use of a given phonetic or phonological feature in its social context in order to understand the linguistic behaviour of members of that social context vis-à-vis that feature. Some L2 speakers, for example, may target the use of [d] for *that* if it is associated with a more urban or street identity whereas others may target [ð] if it is associated with a more educated or upwardly mobile identity.

1.4 The Focus of the Element

While this Element examines a number of social factors in turn, it is important to note that social factors are interconnected – gender is part of identity, for example, and both gender and identity impact and may be impacted by social and peer group networks. How we see ourselves – and how we want others to see us – impacts the way we use language and specific speech features to display our gender, our identity, and social group memberships. Learners may have 'accent aims' (Rindal, 2010), a desire to sound a certain way based on a range of social factors, including exposure to the L2 through study abroad experiences and the mass media, for example. Therefore while the Element necessarily has to discuss each factor separately, connections among factors are made within sections.

Two main lines of research inform the findings outlined in this Element: (1) research on social factors and L2 pronunciation attainment, which usually focuses on *acquisition* of phonetic and phonological features; (2) sociolinguistic variation research on the variable patterns of phonetic and phonology features that are in *use* in the context of the research. In some cases, this research focuses on L2 acquisition while in other cases, on second dialect acquisition – when the acquisition is not of an L2, but of a different dialect, whether an L1 or an L2. This includes speakers of Indian English (IndE), for example, who are learning features of AmE in the United States. While research on the former typically focuses on production of one or more phonetic or phonological features or overall proficiency (or native-like attainment), research on the latter focuses on the acquisition and use of one or more phonetic or phonological features that have several different variants, such as the variable usage of [d] or [ð] as in *that* or *dat*, and the social (and linguistic) factors that constrain usage of each variant. In sum, while L2 acquisition research (area 1) focuses on attainment of a standard or native-like acquisition of the voiced TH, research that focuses on L2 sociolinguistic variation (area 2) would examine the use of [d] versus [ð] among L1 speakers in the community, and the extent to which L2 learners acquire the same [d] versus [ð] variation patterns as L1 speakers in the same community. As an example, if [d] is in wider usage among younger men in the L1 community, the L2 research may focus on whether the younger men in the study have similar patterns of [d] usage, in contrast to older men or younger and older women in the study.

While sociolinguistic variation research has not always been included in traditional accounts of L2 acquisition, findings from this line of research provide insight into how the learner engages with their linguistic environment in terms of which features may be acquired for use. As Clark and Schleef (2010) note, the process of acquiring an L2 is a complex undertaking, as the learner not only has to acquire features of the L2 – such as /d/ and /ð/ – but also has to acquire the variable use patterns in their social context(s); for example, usage of [d] instead of [ð] if variation occurs. This entails awareness that variation exists and that some L1 speakers use [d] and not [ð], as an example. It also entails an understanding of when usage of [d] is more likely to occur, whether this usage is governed by linguistic factors such as the lexical category of the word (article *the* versus a verb *bathe*), word position (onset versus coda – as in *the* versus *bathe*), as well as social categories such as gender (greater usage of [d] by men than women), and age (greater usage by younger versus older speakers). In addition, the L2 learner has to acquire the same social meaning for different variants as members of the L1 community – for example, that [d] is a feature of younger men's speech, possibly to mark a particular identity or social group membership.

Sociolinguistic variation research has found that when contact between two (or more) languages or dialects occurs within a social context that the L2 learner is immersed in, it may result in: (1) use of L1 forms – this is often perceived to be lack of acquisition but may instead be active retention of features from the L1 in order to retain an L1 identity when using the L2; (2) use of L2 forms, often viewed as successful L2 acquisition or pronunciation attainment; or (3) use of a third form – a new phonetic or phonological feature that may be viewed as incomplete learning of the L2 feature. However, this third form may be a new variant that has emerged in the social context to mark a unique L1/L2 identity for a learner or a social group. Nance and colleagues (2016) call this Type 3 variation, in contrast to Type 1 variation (use of L1 forms in place of the L2 form to be acquired, often viewed as 'errors') and Type 2 variation (acquisition of the variation patterns found in the L2). Type 3 variation, in contrast, as Nance and colleagues argue, builds on the supposition that an L2 learner may not aim to sound like a native speaker of the L2, but rather wishes to create a new identity that is distinctive to their own unique language learning and use context. This will be explored throughout the Element.

Along with a broad reading of the literature, this Element attempts to include research from a wide range of languages and learner populations/contexts. To date, much of the research on social factors and L2 phonetics/phonology has focused on the acquisition of English, and for study abroad/immersion studies, French, German, or Spanish. Increasingly, however, research on lesser studied populations and languages is gaining more visibility in the field. This Element includes research focusing on L1 speakers of Arabic, Cantonese, Estonian, Kurdish, Norwegian, Polish, Romanian, and Russian, and L2 learners of Japanese, Scottish Gaelic, and Turkish. It also includes studies from multilingual language use contexts such as Singapore, Malaysia, and Hong Kong, where English may be an L2 or one of several languages learned bilingually or multilingually. Additionally, it includes research in contexts where learners are exposed to different dialects of the L1 and/or L2. This includes studies on the acquisition and use of features of Puerto Rican English versus General American English versus African American Vernacular English, Irish English versus Southern Standard British English (SSBE), Manchester English versus SSBE, Castilian versus Latin American English, and rural versus urban dialects in Syria, among others. While the synthesis of findings discussed in this

Element is based on a broad reading of the available literature, the selection of studies for inclusion was made to represent a range of L2 learning contexts and languages. The Element attempts a balanced overview of all of the social factors, but some factors, including study abroad, have a longer and more robust research tradition, leading to more findings from these lines of research. As a result, while the Element aims for a balanced treatment of all the social factors, the discussion of some factors is more expansive than others.

Sections 2 through 7 of the Element explore different social factors in turn. Through a state-of-the-art synthesis of relevant research, the key findings of how each social factor can impact L2 phonology is discussed. This discussion focuses on both acquisition and use of L2 phonological features.

The discussion of social factors begins with a focus on L2 attitudes, a factor that is not always included in discussions of social factors, as it is often considered to be a cognitive or social psychological factor. This Element, however, examines language attitudes in relation to social group memberships and sociolinguistic stereotypes, and how group memberships and sociolinguistic stereotypes may impact the views of L2 learners towards different varieties of the L2, particularly in settings such as World Englishes contexts, where more than one variety – including a local variety of English – are in use in the environment.

Building upon this discussion, Section 3 examines the impact of social and peer group networks on L2 phonology. This section focuses on the impact of contact with members of different speech communities (including peer group networks and L1 networks) on L2 phonological acquisition and use. Section 4 moves to a focus on learner's interaction with the L2 itself – the learner's L2 contact and exposure. This section includes a discussion of quantity and quality of exposure to the L2 including contact through different modes such as reading and writing, TV, and the Internet. Section 5 extends the discussion of L2 contact and exposure to study abroad experiences. The experiences of students during study abroad (SA) are often contrasted with learners in at home (AH) and/or formal instruction (FI) classroom-based contexts, with a focus not only on how SA experiences can foster L2 pronunciation attainment as well as how these experiences can increase awareness of L2 dialectal variation.

Gender and identity and ethnic group affiliation are then discussed. The discussion of gender focuses on how L1 and/or L2 gender norms and available speech community memberships may impact a learner's access not only to L2 acquisition opportunities but exposure to specific phonological features, which then impacts what the learner may target for acquisition and use. The final social factors discussed in the Element are identity and ethnic group affiliation, as these factors draw together many of the issues raised in the previous discussions of social factors. The discussion of identity examines the learner's views of themself as an L1 and L2 speaker, and how this may impact contact with various L2 and L1 speech communities and, consequently, L2 phonological perception and production. The discussion of ethnic group affiliation extends this discussion to a focus on how ethnic identity impacts the use of L1 and L2 phonological features.

The Element concludes with a discussion of future research directions as well as implications for teaching, addressing the final question posed in the Element: *What are the implications of the social factor findings for teaching L2 pronunciation?* A list of key readings is presented before the reference section.

2 L2 Attitudes

Attitudes towards the L2 are not always included in discussions of social factors as they are considered to be social psychological or cognitive factors and therefore internal rather than social constraints. L2 attitudes is included as a social factor in this Element as it examines the impact of group memberships and sociolinguistic stereotypes on attitudes that L2 learners may form towards different varieties or dialects and/or particular features of the L2 that are associated with a particular social group or community. As such, L2 attitudes are presented as a social factor, part of the relationship that an L2 speaker forms with the language(s) and linguistic features that are in use in different speech communities to which they have access or wish to gain access.

2.1 Defining Language Attitudes

The term 'language ideology' is often used synonymously with language attitudes. As Kroskrity (2016) notes, while both refer to ideas that individuals form about language and language speakers, they have emerged from different disciplines and therefore may best be viewed as complementary rather than interchangeable. Research on language attitudes emerged from the discipline of social psychology in the 1960s, pioneered by Gardner and Lambert and colleagues (see Gardner, 1985; Lambert et al., 1966; Lambert, 1967). Research on language attitudes commonly employ surveys/questionnaires to solicit beliefs and preferences about languages, an approach called a direct approach to the study of language attitudes as participants are asked to self-report attitudes. Another approach is the use of either a matched guise test (MGT) or, more commonly, a verbal guise test (VGT), in which participants are asked to respond to a series of questions about speech samples to which they are asked to listen. In an MGT, one speaker would be recorded speaking in different dialects or languages. The MGT allows for control of other variables, including voice quality. However, as it is difficult to recruit speakers who can speak all the languages or dialects under investigation fluently, researchers more commonly employ a VGT, in which different speakers for each language or dialect under investigation are employed. Listeners are typically asked to assess the speech sample on a Likert scale (usually on a scale from Strongly Agree to Strongly Disagree) based on speaker characteristics such as 'intelligent' and 'educated', and speech attributes, including 'good model of pronunciation'. Both the MGT and the VGT are considered indirect measures of language attitudes as the attitudes are derived from the listener's responses to the series of questions about the speaker and speech (Garrett, 2007).

Language ideologies often examine beliefs about language in relation to power relationships in a given culture. As Woolard (2020) argues, language ideologies are 'morally and politically loaded representations of the nature, structure, and use of languages in a social world' (p. 1) because 'implicitly or explicitly they represent not only how language is, but how it ought to be' (p. 2). The study of language ideologies emerged from the field of linguistic anthropology and is researched through qualitative research methodologies, including ethnographic observation, discourse analysis, and interviews. This Element examines both language attitudes and ideologies under the umbrella term of L2 attitudes.

The study of language attitudes in relation to the acquisition and use of L2 phonetics and phonology has taken three main approaches, primarily within a sociolinguistic research paradigm:

1) The measurement of L2 learner attitudes towards different L2 varieties and dialects, typically using VGTs.
2) The incorporation of language attitude questions or VGT results into a sociolinguistic analysis along with other factors that may impact L2 use. This approach examines the relationship between L2 attitudes and L2 language use.
3) The use of a VGT to solicit L2 learners' attitudes towards specific L2 sociolinguistic variable(s).

While the majority of research on language attitudes in general has focused on the first approach, this Element focuses on the link between L2 attitudes and use of specific phonetic and phonological features of the L2. Therefore, the discussion of language attitudes will primarily focus on approaches 2 and 3. The L2 is not learned in isolation from its social context, and in the process of acquiring the L2, whether in a foreign or a second language setting, L2 learners may form attitudes towards the L2 itself, its culture, and its features.

These attitudes may be influenced by learners' experience living in the target language culture, and/or through exposure to varieties of the L2 via the mass media and classroom instruction. Attitudes towards the L2 may also be influenced by teacher ideologies towards different dialects, and features, of the L2. They have a significant influence on the features of the L2 that learners target or avoid for acquisition or use.

2.2 L2 Attitudes Findings

Before we examine the main findings of this line of research, it is important to note that, as stated in Section 1.3, both awareness of the social meaning of different L2 features as well as the learners' ability to acquire and use targeted L2 features towards a more desired pronunciation impact the effect of social factors on L2 pronunciation acquisition and use. Based on a review of the research, a number of conclusions can be drawn about the impact of attitudes towards the L2, a particular variety of the L2, and features of the L2 on L2 phonetic and phonological acquisition and use. These conclusions are presented in Table 1.

These findings will be discussed in turn, with italics denoting each of the key findings presented in Table 1.

Table 1 A summary of findings on L2 attitudes and L2 phonetics/phonology

- *Attitudes towards specific varieties/dialects may manifest as 'accent aims'; accent aims may correlate with use of specific phonological features associated with that variety.*
- *More positive attitudes towards a variety/dialect, a place, and its culture are associated with greater usage of features associated with that variety.*
- *Negative attitudes towards features of a language or variety may lead to resistance to use of features of that language/variety.*
- *Not all features are impacted equally by attitudes and accent aims; more salient features are used or adopted more frequently than linguistic features that are less salient to learners.*
- *Attitudes may be mitigated by proficiency – learners at a higher proficiency may have increased awareness that different variants exist in a speech community and the social meaning of the use of specific variants.*
- *Teachers' ideologies – often implicit – may shape learners' attitudes towards acquiring and using specific linguistic features.*

- *Attitudes towards specific varieties/dialects may manifest as 'accent aims'; accent aims may correlate with use of specific phonological features associated with that variety.*

A number of studies have found that the positive attitudes L2 learners hold towards a particular variety of an L2 or its features can manifest as 'accent aims', a term Rindal (2010) used to describe the desire L2 learners may have to sound a certain way. In addition, learners may target the use of specific features of the L2 that they perceive to be markers of the L2 accent for which they are aiming.

Research by Rindal (2010) and Rindal and Piercy (2013) as well as my own research (Hansen Edwards, 2016) has focused on the use of AmE versus BrE variants by L2 learners in contexts where BrE has traditionally been the educational model: Norway and Hong Kong. Rindal (2010) focused on four features: postvocalic /r/, intervocalic /t/, and vowels in words in the GOAT and LOT lexical sets. These features distinguish AmE and BrE, along with other Englishes. For example, most varieties of AmE have postvocalic /r/, realization of the 'r' in words such as *car* and *farm*, while most varieties of BrE only have /r/ before a vowel. Intervocalic /t/ is often flapped in AmE (it sounds like a quick 'd' sound as in *sitter* as *sidder*) whereas in BrE it can be aspirated (pronounced with a puff of air) or with a glottal stop (a quick 'uh' sound), called T Glottaling. The vowels in words that belong to the GOAT and LOT lexical sets differ in AmE and BrE (see Appendix).

Along with a production task of a word list and conversation data to record pronunciation of the four features, Rindal (2010) conducted a VGT to elicit attitudes towards AmE and BrE, and collected interview and survey data from twenty-three Norwegian adolescents. She found a positive effect of accent aims on variant usage, with those who stated they aimed for an AmE accent having greater use of AmE features than those who aimed for a BrE accent. As Rindal states, 'This means that not only did learners make choices about desired English pronunciation; they also more or less abided by these choices' (p. 247).

Rindal and Piercy (2013) examined the use of the same linguistic features as Rindal (2010) as well as vowels in the BATH lexical set and post-coronal /j/ among seventy Norwegian adolescent learners of English. Post-coronal /j/ is present in many varieties of BrE after coronal consonants such as /n/ and /t/ and before the vowel /u:/ in words such as *student* and *new.* In contrast, post-coronal /j/ is absent in most varieties of AmE. Along with production data, the researchers asked participants to indicate their L2 accent aims via a questionnaire. While the researchers found a higher usage of AmE variants than BrE variants overall, they found that the use of AmE vs. BrE features was correlated with the learners' desired accent aims: as an example, learners who stated they aimed for an AmE accent used AmE [æ] in words in words in the BATH lexical set, more intervocalic flapping, and more rhoticity than BrE aimers. Conversely, those who aimed for a BrE accent used [ɒ] in LOT more frequently than AmE aimers, and a more BrE pronunciation of GOAT. While the students' accent aims could be influenced by teachers' accents and ideologies about accents, Rindal and Piercy note that in Norway, there are no explicit L2 educational models and variation in the L2 (as well as in Norwegian) is not only tolerated but accepted. It is therefore likely that, as Rindal and Piercy state, students make their own decisions about accent aims.

In research on the use of AmE versus BrE features among speakers of English in Hong Kong, Hansen Edwards (2016) used a reading passage task to solicit use of AmE versus BrE variants for postvocalic /r/, intervocalic /t/, and the LOT and BATH lexical sets vowels. I also elicited accent preferences through a survey task. Similarly to Rindal (2010), I found that the L2 learners' preferences for an AmE accent were associated with the number of AmE variants they used, with higher usage of AmE features among those who preferred AmE. Conversely, a preference for BrE was associated with usage of fewer AmE and more BrE variants. Data from an open-ended question about influences on their accents indicated that participants were aware of accent differences across varieties of English, including between AmE and BrE, and actively aimed to speak with features of their desired accent.

As these studies show, L2 learners are aware of at least some of the features associated with a particular variety of the L2 and may actively target those for L2 acquisition and use based on their desired L2 accent.

- *More positive attitudes towards language or variety, a place, and its culture are associated with greater usage of features associated with that language or variety.*

Research also suggests that positive attitudes towards a particular L2 variety and/or speakers of the L2 variety may increase usage of features that are associated with that variety. Drummond (2010, 2011), for example, conducted research on Polish L1 immigrants to Manchester, England, a multidialectal environment where local features associated with a Manchester accent are in usage along with features from other varieties of BrE. His research focused on attitudes towards Manchester and how this impacted the L2 learners' use of a local Manchester variant, the convergence of the vowels in the STRUT and FOOT lexical sets. This convergence does not exist in SSBE, which is the L2 English educational model the participants in the study were exposed to in Poland. Drummond (2010) found that positive attitudes towards Manchester, a longer length of residence in Manchester, and a native English–speaking partner all favoured use of the STRUT/FOOT convergence. Drummond (2011) also examined whether attitudes towards Manchester were associated with the use of T Glottaling at the ends of words, such as in *lit*, a marker of Manchester

English as well as other Englishes in the United Kingdom. He found that T Glottaling was associated with more positive attitudes towards Manchester, as was a longer length of residence and a higher level of English proficiency. Drummond's research indicates that a positive attitudes towards a place – the region where the L2 features are in use – are associated with adoption of local features.

Research has also focused on learners' attitudes towards the local variant itself, to determine whether more positive attitudes towards a linguistic feature are associated with greater use of the feature. Ringer-Hilfinger (2012) examined dialect acquisition by English L1 speakers of L2 Spanish during a SA experience in Spain. Her research focused on the use of the [s] and [θ] variants of the fricative /s/ in words such *zapato* ('shoe'). In American Spanish, *zapato* is pronounced as *[s]apato* whereas in the northern central dialect to which the students were exposed during the SA, it is pronounced as *[θ]apato*. The author found those with a very positive attitudes towards the use of the [θ] variant by native speakers (NSs) expressed a stronger desire to use this L2 variant.

Research has also examined attitudes towards the L2 language and the L2 culture. In research comparing attitudes towards both in research on immigrant learners in the United States, Moyer (2007) found that while both were linked to higher accent ratings (more native-like accents), L2-related attitudes were more closely related with more native-like accent ratings by NSs of English. Language-related attitudes that were related to both a personal and a professional orientation and outcomes of learning the L2 were statistically significantly closer to native-like accent ratings.

In research on attitudes towards the L2 culture, in this case the attitudes towards American culture by Indian English (IndE) speakers in the United States, Sharma (2005) found that some speakers adopted AmE features. This included post-vocalic /r/ in words such as *car* and *farm* (a non-rhotic realization or a trilled /r/ is more common in IndE); l-velarization, the realization of coda or syllabic /l/ as velarized in words such as *pull* or *hill* (an alveolar realization is more common in IndE); and aspirated voiceless stops in syllables with primary stress as in the first syllables (underlined) in *teacher* and *pastry* (unaspirated stops are more common in IndE). The speakers of IndE who had greater use of the AmE variants expressed a greater interest in accommodating to AmE culture. Positive attitudes to contact with the American culture was a significant factor in the greater use of the three AmE variants – rhoticity, aspiration, and velarization – with those with the most positive attitudes having the greatest use of the AmE variants.

As this research suggests, positive attitudes towards the local region of the L2 use, local features of the L2, and the L2 culture, have all been found to be associated with higher usage of local or variety-specific features. However, as few studies (but see Moyer, 2007) have examined L2 attitudes towards more than one aspect (e.g., attitudes towards the L2 culture or L2), it is unclear whether some attitudes are more influential than others in impacting the L2 learner's accent aims and linguistic choices.

- *Negative attitudes towards features of a variety may lead to resistance to use of features of that language/variety.*

While positive attitudes towards the L2, its features and/or cultures, can manifest in greater usage of features of the L2 and/or variety, research suggests that negative attitudes towards an L2 variety and its features may lead to avoidance of or resistance to usage of features associated with that variety. In research on Polish immigrants to Dublin, Ireland, Diskin and Levey (2019), for example, found that negative attitudes among some immigrants towards Irish English (IrE), and features of IrE including a local Dublin variant of STRUT, led to resistance and/or avoidance in using the local STRUT variant in favour of a SSBE variant of STRUT. One reason for this is that SSBE may be viewed as more prestigious and correct by the learners. In research on attitudes towards features of the L2, Grammon (2021) found that L2 learners of Spanish in the United States avoided the use of a dialectal variant of the L2, the voiceless interdental fricative [θ] (as in *[θ]apato* in the word *zapato* ('shoe')). The learners associated the use of this sound with Castilian Spanish and not the Latin American Spanish they were targeting in their L2 Spanish class in the United States. In research on attitudes towards the L2 culture, Sharma (2005) also found that the IndE speakers with the most negative attitudes to American cultural contact had the lowest rates of usage of rhoticity, aspiration, and l-velarization, features associated with AmE. Taken together with the findings about positive attitudes, these studies indicate that learners form judgments about the L2, features of the L2, and the L2 culture, among others, and that these judgements inform their linguistic choices in terms of which features of the L2 they target for acquisition and use.

- *Not all features are impacted equally by attitudes and accent aims; more salient features are used or adopted more frequently than linguistic features that are less salient to learners.*

Research that has examined several phonetic and/or phonological features has found that some features of the L2 are more likely to be adopted by learners aiming for a particular L2 accent, likely due to the greater salience of some features as markers of a particular variety. Rindal (2010), for example, in research on the AmE versus BrE variants targeted by Norwegian adolescents, found that the most widely used markers for AmE were the AmE variant in the GOAT lexical set, followed by postvocalic /r/, and then the AmE LOT variant, and finally intervocalic flapping. She speculated that the higher prevalence of use of the AmE variant in GOAT by the learners in contrast to other AmE features was due to L1 influence and therefore the relative ease of acquiring the AmE variant by L1 speakers of Norwegian. She posited that the higher prevalence of the use of postvocalic /r/ was likely due to its orthographic influence as well as higher frequency in the input, possibly leading to a higher level of awareness of the use of the /r/ as a feature of an AmE accent. In their research on Norwegian L1 learners of English, Rindal and Piercy (2013) found that use of postvocalic /r/ as well as the AmE variant for GOAT were the most widely used features to mark an AmE accent, followed by intervocalic flapping, and the AmE [æ] in words in the BATH LEXICAL SET. The least widely adopted AmE marker was the AmE variant [ɑ] for words in the LOT lexical set.

In my research (Hansen Edwards, 2016) on Hong Kong L2 learners of English, I found that of the features investigated – postvocalic /r/, intervocalic /t/ flapping versus aspiration, T Glottaling versus aspiration, and vowels in the LOT and BATH lexical sets – the most widely used features of AmE were postvocalic /r/, followed by flapping, and the AmE variant in the BATH lexical set. The use of the AmE variant in the LOT lexical set as well as T Glottaling were used less frequently as markers of an AmE accent. As these three studies suggest, the orthographic salience of 'r' as well as its high frequency of occurrence lexically likely makes this a more salient marker of an AmE accent to L2 learners. It is likely that flapping (vs. aspiration) of intervocalic /t/ is more acoustically and thus perceptually salient to L2 learners as is the differentiation between the low front AmE [æ] versus a low back BrE [ɑː] in words in the BATH lexical set. In contrast, the distinction between the AmE [ɑ] and BrE [ɒ] in words in the LOT lexical set may be less noticeable to learners, given they are both low back vowels and acoustically not as distinctive as the AmE versus BrE variants in BATH.

As these findings suggest, and as discussed earlier, awareness of the existence of different L2 variants is fundamental to the learners' acquisition of a particular variety of a language and/or sociolinguistic competence in that language/variety.

- *Attitudes may be mitigated by proficiency – learners at a higher proficiency may have increased awareness that different variants exist in a speech community and the social meaning of the use of specific variants.*

While variants of more than one feature may exist in the learner's L2 environment, some features – and their variants as well as the social meaning of those variants – may be more salient to the L2 learners and therefore acquired or targeted for use earlier than other features. Awareness of the existence of different L2 variants and their social meaning likely increases with L2 proficiency, as research by Drummond (2010) has found. In his research on L1 Polish immigrants in Manchester, England, Drummond found that learners with a higher proficiency in English had a greater use of the local variant for the STRUT vowel (merged with FOOT in Manchester English).

- *Teachers' ideologies – often implicit – may shape learners' attitudes towards acquiring and using specific linguistic features.*

Finally, what happens in the classroom, and how teachers consciously or subconsciously talk about different varieties of the L2 and features of the L2 varieties, impacts the attitudes learners have towards specific features of the L2, as research by Grammon (2021) found. In a two-year study combining classroom observation of teacher/student interaction with interviews and document analysis on L2 learners of Spanish in the United States, Grammon found that L2 learners had formed ideologies about the use of the voiceless interdental fricative [θ] (*[θ]apato*), a dialectal variant of Castilian Spanish, based on the statements expressed about the use of [θ] by their classroom teacher. These included normative and prescriptive statements about the use of [θ], that students should learn Latin American Spanish rather than Castilian Spanish, and that variety mixing was not encouraged. As Grammon stated, the students internalized these beliefs and thus avoided using [θ], thus limiting their own sociolinguistic development.

Although research on L2 attitudes has not always been included in discussions of social factors and L2 pronunciation, the findings highlighted in this section indicate that learners' attitudes towards an L2 variety, its culture, and its features, impact their adoption of features that they perceive to be markers of the L2 variety. This underscores the agency learners have in L2 acquisition and use, as well as their awareness of varietal or dialectal differences in the L2, and can help explain diverse accent aims and learning outcomes among L2 learners. Social and peer group networks also influence what learners target in the L2 for acquisition and use; this will be explored in more detail in Section 3.2.

3 Social and Peer Group Networks

3.1 Defining Social and Peer Group Networks

A main line of research on social factors and phonetics and phonology is the impact of social and peer group networks on L2 acquisition and use. This line of research focuses on the impact of with whom the L2 learner engages during L2 acquisition and use. Research on social networks (SNs) in L2 acquisition and use has emerged from L1 dialectology and sociolinguistic research paradigms and has built upon work on language change in dialects by J. Milroy and L. Milroy, who pioneered the concepts of social network size and density (see for example Milroy & Milroy, 1985, 1992) to examine how (and why) some linguistic features diffuse among members of a particular community. Gender is a key element of their Social Network Theory. This will be examined in more detail in Section 6.2. Milroy and Milroy (1992) proposed that individual's SNs comprise a 'web of ties' to other people. SNs can be further defined as 'close knit' – dense and multiplex – wherein individuals are known to others (density) in a range of ways (multiplicity). In an SN that has maximal density, everyone in the network would know everyone else; for networks that are maximally multiplex, individuals would know each other from a range of settings, such as through work, school, the gym, and religious meetings. SNs can also be relatively open, in communities where there is a lot of population movement. Language innovation and change is posited to occur in loose-knit network structures as these structures are more permeable to contact with individuals from other SNs, through which new linguistic features may be introduced. In contrast, closer-knit networks may lead to less linguistic innovation. SN theory has been widely adopted by both L1 and L2 researchers as it provides a useful way of examining language innovation and change in communities, as well as the use of specific L2 features among L2 learners. The social and peer group networks to which the L2 learner belongs or wishes to belong exert a significant influence on the pronunciation features that the learner targets for acquisition and use as linguistic features are an important means through which individuals can mark and display social memberships. Learners may also target non-standard and/or local features of the L2 if these features are in usage among the social networks or peer groups to which they belong or wish to gain access.

3.2 Social and Peer Group Networks Findings

Research on SNs has focused on a range of social ties, including family, workplace, and peer group networks. In research on peer group networks, the focus is often on child or adolescent learners, as the primary influences on younger learners' language use may be friends or classmates in the immediate environment, in contrast to adults, who may have a wider range of social contacts through extended family, work, or study opportunities, among others. Findings emerging from research in L2 phonetics and phonology are presented in Table 2. These will be discussed in detail in this sub-section, with examples drawn from relevant research to elucidate the findings.

Table 2 A summary of findings on social and peer networks and L2 phonetics/phonology

- *Diversity, density, and size of the learners' social network are all important.*
- *Successful social networks may lead to acculturation success, and L2 pronunciation attainment.*
- *Peer group networks or peer culture affiliation are important for L2 identity formation, and consequently, for L2 acquisition and use. L2 learners may target the features in use among their peer group, to signal belonging to that social group or an aspiration to belong to that social group, even if these features are non-standard.*
- *Peer group networks may begin having a strong influence on learners at a young age.*
- *Gender and friendship/peer social networks are often intertwined and what may be interpreted as gender-based differences can be due to use of some norms associated with a particular peer network.*

These findings are discussed here.

- *Diversity, density, and size of the learners' social network are all important.*

Research suggests that various dimensions of SNs influence the learner's adoption of L2 features in use among members of their social network(s). In addition, SNs may influence a range of L2 features, including development of socio-phonetic variation patterns and increased oral proficiency and fluency in the L2. Sharma (2011), for example, found that the diversity of the learners' SNs is important, as this can impact the acquisition and use of socio-phonetic variants. In research on first- and second-generation Punjab Indians in Southall, a suburb of London, Sharma (2011) adopted an SN Diversity Index as most of the participants in her study had primarily Asian network ties. The Diversity Index was created based on a range of factors, including the number of contacts, which was defined as the number of acquaintances, friends, and relatives. Other factors included the frequency and domains of interaction (multiplexity) in the SN, the shared ties within the SN (density), the dialect and ethnicity of each contact in the SN, and relative closeness ranking for each contact in the SN. Each contact was then categorized into a sub-group such as family, friend, or coworker. In addition, two dimensions were measured by the Diversity Index – the number of individuals per sub-group and the total number of sub-groups.

Sharma's (2011) research focused on several features, including the realization of /t/ as in *ṯan*. This may be realized as a retroflex voiceless stop [ʈ] in IndE and is a salient marker of this variety. In most varieties of BrE, /t/ is realized as the voiceless alveolar stop [t]. She found that both gender and age differences existed in the use of the retroflex [ʈ] as older men and younger women had a great deal more style shifting between use of the retroflex IndE and the alveolar BrE variant, in contrast to younger men and older women, who had greater use of [ʈ]. Sharma argued that the greater use of retroflex by younger men and older women was because they were more invariant in their SNs. Older women used more retroflex [ʈ] than younger women due to primarily Asian social networks within the community, and younger men used a hybrid style with features of both IndE and other BrE varieties due to British Asian friendships. In contrast, younger women and older men had more diverse SNs across communities, with ties in both Asian (home, friends) and British (work) networks, and therefore more interactions among diverse groups, leading to more shifting between the IndE and BrE realizations of /t/ for these two groups in comparison to older women and younger men.

Kennedy Terry (2017, 2022) also conducted research on the effect of different dimensions of SNs on the acquisition of sociolinguistic variation of French /l/, which is deleted in third-person subject clitic pronouns, among L1 speakers of English learning French. For example, *elle m'a dit* ('she told me') can be pronounced as [ɛl ma di] or with /l/ elision as [ɛ ma di] (see Kennedy Terry, 2017, p. 558). She used a Social Network Strength Scale, which consisted of two density and two multiplexity measures: Density Measure 1 measured the number of NSs of French with whom each learner spoke French for minimally thirty minutes per week while Density Measure 2 measured the interrelations among the NSs listed as part of Density Measure 1. Multiplexity Measure 1 was a measure of the number of different activities the learner engaged in with each of the NSs in Density Measure 1 as well as the number of other NSs not listed with whom they engaged regularly. Multiplexity Measure 2 focused on the topics of conversation between the learner and the NSs. Kennedy Terry found that lower overall scores on the Social Network Strength Scale were associated with lower rates of /l/ deletion, indicating the ability to develop varied SNs and engage in a range of activities with members of these SNs fosters the acquisition of L2 socio-phonetic patterns during SA.

In a study on with the same participants as the 2017 study, Kennedy Terry (2022) found that the most significant predictor of the acquisition of French /l/ variation patterns were Social Network Strength Scores. In addition, she found that these findings were consistent across linguistic variables as she also examined the acquisition of schwa deletion patterns among the L2 learners of French and found similar results: higher Social Network Strength Scores were correlated with higher rates of schwa deletion, and a closer approximation to the socio-phonetic variation patterns of NSs of French.

Along with the diversity of the SN, the more social groups to which the learner belongs and the closer the learner is to members of these social groups may also impact L2 proficiency gains, as may size of the SNs. Baker-Smemoe, Dewey, Bown, and Martinsen (2014) examined L2 gains made by 102 students of L2 Spanish, Chinese, French, Russian, and Arabic going on SA programmes. They measured oral L2 gains through an oral proficiency interview and SNs through a Social Interaction Questionnaire, the latter of which focused on the size, durability, density, and dispersion of the students' SNs. Size was defined as the number of NSs in the learner's network while durability was defined as frequency of interaction with each person in the learner's network. Intensity was defined as the degree of closeness the learner felt they had with each member of their network, density was defined as how close the members of the SN were, and dispersion was defined as the number of groups in which the learner participated. In addition, the study examined the English proficiency of the members in a learner's network. These factors were compared for the students who were categorized as gainers (significant oral proficiency gains in the SA experience) versus non-gainers, with results showing that the learners who had greater gains in oral proficiency belonged to more social groups (greater dispersion) and had closer relationships with members of these social groups (greater intensity). Another factor was significant: a decrease in the size of the learners' SNs during the SA experience. The authors posit that smaller networks may lead to higher quality and quantity of L2 usage, potentially due to the closer friendships formed in the smaller networks, and that this higher quality and quantity of L2 usage promotes L2 oral proficiency gains.

Bejarano, Dewey, Baker-Smemoe, Henrichsen, and Hall (2019) examined oral fluency gains and SN development during an SA experience using the Study Abroad Social Interaction Questionnaire. This measured five variables: size (the number of people in the SN), durability (frequency of association of each person in the SN), intensity (average closeness with each member of the SN), Density 1 (the size of the largest social group), Density 2 (the average size of the social groups), and dispersion (the number of social groups listed). Fluency was measured through speech task and rated by NSs. Bejarano and colleagues found that SNs were significant, and in particular, the number of NSs of the L2 within the SN as well as dispersion within the SN, indicating that having a large network of speakers of the target language fostered L2 fluency gains. This appears to contradict findings by Baker-Smemoe and colleagues (2014), who found that having smaller SNs led to higher quality L2 use, which may foster oral proficiency gains. However, the studies measured different features – overall oral proficiency versus L2 fluency – and it is likely that various aspects of the L2 benefit from different types of interaction. This requires more research. Overall, however, the research suggests that the development of SNs with L2 speakers through which L2 speakers can engage in meaningful L2 use fosters the development of socio-phonetic awareness and competence as well as L2 proficiency and fluency gains.

- *Successful social networks may lead to acculturation success, and L2 pronunciation attainment.*

The development of stronger L2 SNs may also support acculturation and foster L2 pronunciation gains. Work by Lybeck (2002) on American L1 speakers of English in Norway explored the impact of SNs on acculturation patterns, and the association among these with the realization of /r/ (*run, right*) (realized as trill or tap in Norwegian and an alveolar approximant in AmE), and overall L2 pronunciation attainment. Lybeck found that the American women who had been able to develop supportive SNs in Norway had greater usage of the Norwegian /r/ in contrast to AmE /r/, and had a higher Norwegian L2 attainment than those who did not develop supportive social networks. The women who made the greatest gains were those who had both family ties to Norwegians through marriage and were also able to create their own separate Norwegian SNs. In contrast, those who were less successful only had supportive SNs through marriage. Least successful were those who had few supportive networks in Norway. These three SN patterns fostered different acculturation patterns, with those with multiple SNs having greater levels of acculturation, Norwegian /r/ use, and Norwegian pronunciation attainment. In contrast, those with the least supportive SNs had the greatest use of the AmE /r/ in contrast to the Norwegian /r/ and lower levels of L2 pronunciation attainment. In research on English as a second language (ESL) learners in the United States from various L1 backgrounds, including Portuguese, Polish, Bantu, Hindi, and Hebrew, Moyer (2011) found that interaction with NS friends, as well as Length of Residence (LOR, see Section 4) were the most significant predictors of more native-like accentedness ratings, which were done by NSs of English. It is also likely that more successful L2 SNs and acculturation fosters the L2 learners' desire to sound more like a native-speaker of the L2 and develop a viable L2 identity as a speaker of the L2 (see Section 7).

- *Peer group networks or peer culture affiliation are important for L2 identity formation, and consequently, for L2 acquisition and use. L2 learners may target the features in use among their peer group, to signal belonging to that social group or an aspiration to belong to that social group, even if these features are non-standard.*

Research has focused on the impact that peer group networks have on L2 acquisition and use, particularly among adolescents who may have access to several different peer groups and use particular L2 (or L1) features to signal membership in one of these groups.

An early study by Anisman (1975) on Puerto Rican male adolescents learning English L2 in New York City focused on the use of different variants among three main peer groups: African American peers, Puerto Rican peers, and mainstream peers. The features examined included the voiced TH (*that*), the PRICE vowel /aɪ/, and the schwa (a weak vowel in some varieties of English, as in the second syllable of *comma*). As an example, the use of [d] for the voiced TH (*that* as *dat*) is a marker of African American Vernacular English (AAVE). Anisman found greater usage of [d], along with other AAVE variants, among the adolescents who had stronger African American peer group networks. In contrast, more Spanish variants were in use among those who had stronger Puerto Rican networks, including the realization of PRICE with a more tense articulation and realization of voiced TH as [ð], the prestige variant in Puerto Rican Spanish. Finally, those who were targeting mainstream norms had more Standard AmE variants.

In research on adolescent Romanian immigrants to Manchester, England, Howley (2015) examined the acquisition and use of the weak vowel in words in the *HAPPY* (lowered and backed in Manchester English compared with SSBE), and the *LETTER* (lowered and backed in Manchester English compared with SSBE) lexical sets. Howley categorized the peer friendship groups of his 27 participants, who were aged 11–16, into five groups: G1, who had all Roma friends; G2, who had little mixing but some had non-Roma friends; G3, who had somewhat mixed though mostly Roma friends; G4, who were more mixed, but closest friends were Roma; and G5, whose closest friends were non-Roma. He categorized the G1–G3 SNs as closed, as they were primarily Roma; the G4–G5 SNs were classified as open, as these networks included non-Roma friends. He found that those who had more open non-Roma SNs (G4 and G5) had a local Manchester *LETTER* pronunciation in contrast to those with closed – and more Roma – networks (G1–G3); for the *HAPPY* vowel, adolescents in the closed (G1–G3) networks only had a non-Manchester realization of the final vowel whereas those with open (G4–G5) networks had both the local as well as a more standard BrE realization of the vowel. The use of GOOSE-fronting, the articulation of the vowel in the GOOSE lexical set as a more centralized or fronted vowel, which is emerging as a supralocal variant in the United Kingdom and a local feature of

Manchester English, was found to be more prevalent among those with local G4–G5 peer group networks, as well as among female rather than male adolescents (see more in Section 4). In research on Polish teenage immigrants to London and Edinburgh, Schleef, Meyerhoff, and Clark (2011) found that the Polish teenagers in Edinburgh with Scottish or mixed networks in contrast to more Polish networks, had greater use of the local variant [ɪn] for the suffix (ing) (as in *swimming* as *swimmin', running* as *runnin'*) in contrast to the more standard variant [ɪŋ].

As these studies show, L2 learners may not only be aware of how linguistic features are used in the social/peer groups in their communities, but they are also able to use the features in use among their preferred social/peer groups to enact a linguistic identity in line with the norms of their preferred social/peer groups.

- *Peer group networks may begin having a strong influence on learners at a young age.*

Research has found that even learners at a young age are influenced by language use patterns in their peer group networks. Nance (2020), for example, examined the use of Gaelic versus English aspirated/voiceless stops (voiceless stops in Gaelic are pre-aspirated in contrast to English stops, which have aspiration post stop release) as well as /l/ (as in *balach* 'boy', *baile* 'town', and *Cailleach* 'old woman'), which has three realizations in Scottish Gaelic, among children aged seven to eleven. While Nance did not find differences among the children in their realization of voiceless stops and the laterals based on home language (English vs. Gaelic), she did find differences between the children and the adolescents/adults in the same community, particularly with regard to the lack of a difference in alveolar and palatalized laterals, which appear merged for the children but not for adults and adolescents. Interestingly, even the children who had Gaelic as a home language had the same patterns for laterals as the non-Gaelic dominant children. Nance posited that the children had developed their own unique 'community of practice' in their Gaelic language class as only one Gaelic language class was available in the children's community and all the children attended the same class. She suggests that the children were orienting towards peer group models even at the age of 7, indicating that even young children begin making evaluations of the social meaning of different variants. For Multicultural London English (MLE), a variety of BrE used in multi-ethnic regions of London, research by Cheshire, Kerswill, Fox, and Torgersen (2011) found that MLE speech norms were acquired by younger non-Anglo children (ages four to five) from their peers as their caretakers did not use the MLE features that the children were adopting. These studies suggest that socio-phonetic awareness is acquired at an early age and stage of L2 or second dialect acquisition.

- *Gender and peer social networks are often intertwined and what may be interpreted as gender-based differences can be due to use of some norms associated with a particular peer network.*

In research on teenage Polish L1 immigrants in London and Edinburgh, Meyerhoff and Schleef (2012) focused on a range of social factors, including L2 attitudes (see also Section 2) and friendship/peer group networks, and the acquisition of the variable usage of (ing), the suffix found on verbs and gerunds such as *swimming, running*. This has two realizations – a local variant [ɪn] (*swimmin'*) and a standard variant [ɪŋ] (*swimming*). The researchers compared the Polish teenagers' variable use of (ing) and the social and linguistic rules that appeared to govern this usage with NSs of English in Edinburgh and London, to examine the extent to which the Polish teenagers had acquired local variation patterns for the suffix. While linguistic constraints were the most significant factor in realization of (ing) for both the London and Edinburgh Polish teens, in Edinburgh, peer group network was the second strongest constraint, with the Polish teens who had either mainly Scottish or mixed peer networks having greater use of the local variant [ɪn]. In London, gender was the strongest social constraint on (ing) usage and ranked as the third most significant constraint for Polish teens. The researchers suggest that the findings from Edinburgh on the effects of peer group networks and from London on gender are in fact illustrative of the same processes given that friendship networks may be gendered. Sharma's (2011) research on style shifting between IndE and BrE variants of /t/ among older and younger Punjab Indians in London also suggest that the development of diverse SNs is gendered. This will be explored in more detail below (see Section 6).

As these studies show, it is not only the ability to develop SNs with L2 speakers that fosters acquisition of the L2 and development of socio-phonetic competence in the L2, but the interaction that happens within the SNs that is important. Having a higher quality of interaction with members of the SN and more diverse SNs fosters L2 gains. In addition, peer group networks exert a powerful effect on the L2 phonetic and phonological features that L2 learners target for acquisition and use even if these features are non-standard. This is likely because pronunciation features are an important means through which individuals signal group memberships (see also Section 7). Even young children appear to be influenced by peer group networks and may target features in use among their peer groups even if these features are not in use among their parents. The findings on social peer group networks (see Section 3) focused on the impact of *whom* the learners interact with for L2 acquisition and use. The discussion of L2 contact and exposure (see Section 4) extends this focus to an examination of *how* the learner engages with the L2 through an analysis of the quality and quantity of the contact the learner has with the L2 and speakers of the L2.

4 L2 Contact and Exposure

4.1 Defining L2 Contact and Exposure

The ways in which learners engage with the L2 itself is also important. Early research focused on Length of Residence, or LOR, as a measure of learners' contact with the target language, with the finding that a longer LOR was associated with a more native-like pronunciation in the L2 (Purcell & Suter 1980; Suter 1976; Thompson 1991). This operationalization of L2 contact is problematic, however, for several key reasons: (1) LOR is often confounded with another variable, Age of Arrival (AOA), as learners with a longer LOR have often arrived in the L2 culture at a younger age; and (2) residence in the target language culture does not equate with actual L2 exposure and use. More recently, LOR has been defined as the extent of L2 and L1 use, and/or L2 experience. This line of research has found that decreased use of the L1 and greater use of the L2 may foster more native-like accentedness ratings in the L2. Conversely higher L1 use may be a predictor of a stronger L2 accent (Piske, MacKay & Flege 2001). L1 usage while in the L2 culture may limit the learner's opportunities to engage in the type of L2 use that fosters L2 pronunciation gains. In addition, the quality of the experience the L2 learner has with the L2 is significant – exposure to the L2 in and of itself may not foster L2 gains. Rather, sustained usage of the L2 across a range of modes and contexts is an important factor in fostering L2 pronunciation gains.

4.2 L2 Contact and Exposure Findings

In this Element, the focus is on the level of authentic engagement the learner has with the L1 and L2 culture. For this reason, the term 'L2 contact and exposure' is used to emphasize a focus on the level of active engagement the learner has with the L2 (and L1). Key conclusions drawn from the research surveyed are presented in Table 3. Each of these is then discussed, along with references to research that supports each conclusion. A great deal of this research has focused on L2 pronunciation gains either in terms of overall oral proficiency or L2 accuracy, with a few studies examining acquisition of phonetic features of different varieties of the L2.

Table 3 A summary of findings on language contact and exposure and L2 phonetics/phonology

- *L1 use (relative to L2 use) and L2 use can both impact L2 pronunciation gains.*
- *Type and quantity of L2 contact and exposure are both important for L2 pronunciation gains.*
- *Mass media exposure may override educational influences in impacting which L2 features are targeted or acquired.*
- *L2 pronunciation features may be affected differentially by L2 contact and exposure.*

These findings are discussed below.

- *L1 use (relatively to L2 use) and L2 use can both impact L2 pronunciation gains.*

As noted previously, while early research primarily focused on the effect of the amount of L2 use on L2 pronunciation accuracy and gains, later research has examined L1 as well as L2 use. Findings indicate both L1 and L2 use impacts gains in the L2. Research on immigrants learning L2 German by Moyer (2004), for example, found that learners themselves believed that amount of L2 contact impacted their L2 success. Moyer found that these effects may be mitigated by age, as younger immigrants appeared to more easily establish L2 networks that provided opportunities for L2 use, in contrast to older learners, who may have had more difficulty developing L2 social contacts. L1 use was viewed by the immigrants as interfering with L2 development and cultural assimilation, indicating that the immigrants were actively resisting and avoiding L1 use in order to make greater gains in the L2. Moyer's findings also suggest that age should be investigated as a social variable that limits and fosters L2 learners' development of social opportunities for meaningful L2 use. This is explored in more detail shortly. Moyer (2011), in research on ESL learners in the United States from different backgrounds, found that extent of L1 use was correlated with a less native-like accent in the L2. Stevens (2011), in research on Spanish L2 learners, found that L1 use (English) was negatively correlated with L2 vowel accuracy: students with lower rates of L1 usage had higher accuracy in the production of L2 Spanish vowels, in contrast to students with higher rates of L1 usage. Trimble (2013), in research on the acquisition of L2 Spanish suprasegmental patterns, found that greater gains were associated with less L1 English and more L2 Spanish usage. It is likely that higher rates of L1 usage may reduce the students' opportunities to use the L2, thus impacting their L2 development opportunities.

While L2 use with target-language speakers appears to foster L2 pronunciations, L2 use with other learners of the L2 may negatively impact L2 development, underscoring the importance of whom the learners engage with in the L2 (see also Section 3). Alvord and Christensen (2012) focused on the acquisition of Spanish spirantization of /b d g/, a process in which these consonants are produced as voiced approximants [β ð ɣ] as in *b̲ota* /b̲ota/ ('boot') realized as [β̲o.ta]. Spirantization has been found to be difficult for L2 learners of Spanish to acquire. Alvord and Christensen found that the students, all of whom had been living in a Spanish-speaking country for two years, were able to acquire native-like patterns for spirantization for /b d g/, but that the more they spoke L2 Spanish with another English NS (a speaker of the same L1), the less native-like their pronunciation of the spirants. This may be due to greater exposure to other L2 learners' Spanish rather than Spanish of NSs. The former may provide the students with L2 pronunciation models that differ from those taught – and assessed – in the L2 classroom.

In research on younger (mean age 20.5) and older (mean age 53.74) L1 speakers of Estonian, Ader and Miljan (2015) found that more frequent monthly communication with NSs of English had a positive effect on L2 accents, and that the younger L2 learners of English outperformed the older learners overall. In contrast to Alvord and Christensen (2012), Ader and Miljan found also that frequency of communication in the L2 with other learners of the L2 had a positive impact for older learners (it did not impact the younger learners as few differences for this variable existed within this group), indicating that for the older group, speaking the L2 was beneficial, regardless of whether they spoke with NSs or other L2 learners. The findings about younger and older learners provide interesting insights into age as a factor in L2 acquisition. Age is typically viewed as a biological variable and widely perceived to have a significant effect on native-like pronunciation attainment, with native-like pronunciation hypothesized to be attainable only for L2 learners before the critical period, which is posited to exist before the onset of puberty. Ader and Miljan's findings, as well as those of Moyer (2004), discussed in Section 4.2, suggest that social factors – and in particular the ability to form successful social networks in the L2 – may differ between younger and older learners, and can help explain why younger learners are able to attain more accurate or native-like pronunciation abilities in the L2 than older learners. In other words, age may be an important variable in L2 pronunciation attainment because it can limit learners' abilities to develop and sustain the types of L2 contact and exposure opportunities that enable the learner to attain more accurate or native-like L2 pronunciation. This suggests that age may at least partially be a social variable as it may impact learners' abilities to create viable social networks with L2 speakers, which are important in fostering L2 pronunciation attainment. These findings also indicate that for some learner groups, L2 practice – regardless of with whom the learners engage – is beneficial. As the studies suggest, older learners, in particular, may benefit from increased L2 usage regardless of with whom they engage in this usage.

- *Type and quantity of L2 contact and exposure are both important for L2 pronunciation gains.*

As discussed, L2 use, particularly with NSs of the L2, has been found to foster L2 pronunciation gains. Research has also examined the type and quantity of L2 (and L1) use, to determine whether some types of L2 use are more beneficial to pronunciation attainment than others. Moyer (2011) has focused on L2 experience, which she defines as 'active language practice and use' (p. 194). Her research operationalized this to focus both on quantity of L2 experience (amount of type and quantity of modes) as well as quality of the L2 experience (the extent to which the learner engages in L2 use in 'functionally significant ways' p. 195). Moyer conducted research on ESL learners in the United States from different L1 backgrounds. While Moyer did not find that *quantity* of L2 use led to greater L2 pronunciation accuracy, the *quality* of the L2 use did. Specifically, she found that the learners who engaged or interacted with the L2 in multiple modes – through speaking, listening, writing, and reading – as well as in both more formal and informal settings, had more native-like accentedness ratings. Interaction with NS friends was a strong predictor of native-like accentedness ratings, as was a longer LOR. In an earlier study on immigrants to Berlin who were learning L2 German, Moyer (2004) found that the frequency with which the immigrants spoke German with NSs was correlated with nativeness ratings, with the higher frequency of interaction correlated with more native-like ratings.

Research (Alvord & Christensen, 2012) on American men on SA programmes in Spanish-speaking countries also found that greater engagement with the L2 led to greater L2 pronunciation gains, finding that the more time the learners spent studying Spanish, the greater their pronunciation gains. In his research on the acquisition of L2 Spanish suprasegmental patterns, Trimble (2013) found that those who had made greater L2 intonation gains towards more native-like patterns had significantly more interaction with NSs of Spanish than those who made fewer intonation gains.

Research by Kissling (2014) on L2 Spanish learners illustrates that what learners do outside the L2 classroom – with whom they interact and in which language/dialect/variety they engage – impacts their L2 pronunciation attainment. She found that the L2 learners who had less interaction in Spanish outside the L2 classroom made greater gains in an explicit pronunciation class in Spanish than those who interacted more in Spanish outside the classroom. Kissling speculated that one cause for this may be the interaction with non-standard speakers of Spanish outside the classroom, through which the learners may have acquired non-standard variants (see also Section 3), which they may have used more frequently than the standard variants learned in class. Learners with less exposure to L2 Spanish outside the classroom, in contrast, may only have acquired the standard variants, leading to greater (perceived) gains in Spanish as measured by accuracy measures based on a standard pronunciation model.

In research on the attainment in L2 accent by immigrants to Germany in different age groups, Dollman, Kogan, and Weißmann (2020) found that increased exposure to NSs can mitigate the effects of age on L2 accents, finding that stronger accents were correlated with AOA, with those arriving in Germany after the age of ten having a stronger accent than those arriving before that age, and those arriving after the age of sixteen having the strongest accents. However, each month of being with a native German speaking partner, increased usage of German with family and friends, and an increase in the number of NS Germans in the immediate neighbourhood of the immigrant, were associated with a less noticeable foreign accent, indicating that increased exposure could increase native-like attainment for adolescent and adult L2 learners. These findings support the conclusions drawn from research by Ader and Miljan (2015) and Moyer (2004) that age as a factor in L2 pronunciation attainment may be at least partially explained by the ways in which age can limit or foster the ability to form relationships with speakers of the L2, with younger learners often having more opportunities through school and other activities than older learners. As a result, younger learners are able engage in the types of interactions and rich exposure to L2 input that foster L2 gains, in contrast to older adults, who may have more limited social networks. Gender may also have an effect on the development of social networks through which learners may have opportunities to engage in the types of interactions that foster socio-phonetic development and L2 pronunciation gains (see the studies by Hansen Edwards (2009) and Sharma (2011), discussed in Section 6).

Finally, research also suggests that L2 contact impacts the development of successful communication strategies, which, in turn, may impact L2 proficiency and fluency gains. In research on SA and AH L2 learners of English from the United States, Segalowitz, Freed, Collentine, Lafford, Lazar, and Díaz-Campos (2004) found that the amount of contact L2 learners have with Spanish NSs during an SA experience impacted the number of communication strategies employed by students: the greater the contact, the fewer the communication strategies used. As they note, this indicated that greater level of L2 use during the SA increased the students' abilities to bridge communication gaps and successfully communicate with NSs. The SA students outperformed the AH students in oral proficiency gains as well as on oral fluency measures such as rate of speech, longest fluent run (free of hesitations and fillers), and mean length of filler-free runs. The authors argue that the SA students' developed 'superior narrative discourse abilities' (p. 13) during the SA due to the increased opportunities to engage with NSs during the SA, which led to greater oral fluency and proficiency gains for the SA students than the AH students.

- *Mass media exposure may override educational influences in impacting which L2 features are targeted or acquired.*

Exposure to a range of L2 accents and varieties of a language through the mass media has also been found to impact learners' accent aims as well as their use of different linguistic features. In some cases, the exposure students have to a range of accents via the mass media may have a more dominant effect on the learners' L2 accent than the educational models to which students are exposed in the classroom.

In a study of Norwegian L1 learners of English, Rindal (2010) and Rindal and Piercy (2013) found that while there was a greater usage of AmE variants among the Norwegian adolescents who aimed for an AmE accent, there was widespread usage of some AmE variants among all the adolescents. The participants stated that their use of AmE features was influenced by the high level of exposure to AmE accents through the American mass media relative to other varieties of English, such as BrE. The researchers therefore posited that the widespread usage of AmE features was due to the exposure the adolescents had to AmE through the mass media. Even those learners who aimed for a BrE accent were found to have a considerable number of features of AmE in their speech. In my own research (Hansen Edwards, 2016), I found that while use of AmE variants was higher among Hong Kong university students who preferred an AmE over a BrE accent, features of AmE, and particularly rhoticity and flapping, were found across almost all of the participants of the study, even among those who expressed a strong preference for BrE. I suggested that increasing access to AmE as well as the global domination of AmE media (Bielby & Harrington, 2008) is increasing exposure, and subsequently adoption of AmE features even in contexts that have traditionally been BrE-dominant.

A number of studies focusing on Singapore supports these conclusions. In an early study, Hiang and Gupta (1992) found a higher usage of postvocalic /r/ (*car*, *farm*) among younger speakers as well as those who had a higher level of exposure to American media. Poedjosoedarmo (2000) found rhoticity, flapping (*sitter* as *sidder*), and the AmE variant [æ] rather than the BrE [ɑː] in words in the BATH lexical set among Singaporean university students. She suggested exposure to AmE accents through mass media led to the usage of AmE features in this former British colony. Tan (2012) examined the emergence of rhoticity in SgE and found the use of the postvocalic /r/ was higher among tertiary students from a higher socio-economic background. She suggests this is due to increased exposure to American media among university students from these backgrounds.

L2 learners are exposed to different dialects/variants of the L2 outside the classroom, through peers and social networks and the mass media. Through this exposure, learners may develop more positive attitudes towards particular accents and acquire features of the L2 that they perceive as linguistic markers of these accents, even if these are different from what is taught in the L2 classroom or in use by their parents.

- *L2 pronunciation features may be affected differentially by L2 contact and exposure.*

As the preceding discussion on language attitudes (see Section 2) and social and peer group networks (see Section 3) has shown, differences exist in which features are targeted for acquisition and use in contexts where multiple variants occur, probably due to the greater frequency and perceptual prominence of some phonetic and phonological features over others. Similarly, research suggests all L2 features do not benefit equally from greater L2 contact and exposure.

In research on the acquisition of English suprasegmental features among L2 immigrants to Canada, Trofimovich and Baker (2006) found that greater L2 exposure facilitated development of more native-like stress-timing patterns among the learners, but did not impact speech rate, pause frequency, and pause duration. Derwing, Munro, and Thomson (2007) conducted a longitudinal study across ten months for Russian and Mandarin Chinese speakers learning English. Greater gains in fluency were found for those with greater contact with L2 speakers while degree of accentedness was not impacted by L2 contact. The researchers found that greater gains in fluency were made by the Russian L1 language speakers, possibly due to the establishment of more L2 SNs. In contrast, the Mandarin Chinese speakers had more L1 networks, and fewer L2 networks, leading to fewer opportunities for L2 contact outside the classroom.

As these studies suggest, it may be that some suprasegmental features are more likely to be impacted by naturalistic exposure to the L2 than others, and that segmental features are less likely to be impacted by naturalistic exposure.

This has important implications for language assessment as well as research on the acquisition of L2 features, as gains in some aspects of the L2 may be overlooked if the focus of the assessment and/or research is on a feature that is more difficult to acquire. In addition, L1 use may limit learners' opportunities to engage in the types of interactions that foster L2 pronunciation gains. In contrast, L2 learners who engage in a higher quantity of L2 use across a range of modes and with diverse speakers (see also Section 3) achieve more L2 pronunciation gains than learners who have more L1 use or engage less in the L2. L2 use with target-language speakers appears particularly beneficial for accuracy gains. In contrast, L2 use with other learners of the L2 may be less beneficial for L2 pronunciation accuracy, probably because L2 use with L2 learners may expose learners to and further ingrain non-standard features that may be viewed as 'errors' in standard assessments. However, for some learner populations, such as older learners in the target-language context, any L2 use is beneficial, as these learner populations may be less able to develop networks of NSs of the L2 with whom to engage. The findings from this line of research also suggests that age should be viewed at least partially as a social variable that fosters or limits learners' opportunities to engage in meaningful L2 use. Studying abroad is another means through which L2 learners have access to meaningful L2 use opportunities. This is explored in Section 5.

5 Study Abroad

5.1 Defining Study Abroad

Study abroad refers to a temporary stay in the L2 context, usually as part of a secondary or university programme to foster L2 development. The stay in the L2 context typically lasts several months to one year. Research in this area may compare learners who are undergoing SA with students who are 'at home' (AH), either receiving no instruction or receiving formal classroom-based instruction of the foreign language (referred to as formal instruction, FI), or in an intensive immersion (IM) (sometimes called 'intensive summer immersion' as the programme is usually offered during the summer). IM programmes usually consist of all-day domestic immersion in the L2 through classroom instruction in the AH setting. Research on SA is robust, particularly in the United States where many SA programmes are offered for the study of L2 German, French, and Spanish.

As with research on L2 contact and exposure (see Section 4), SA research typically focuses on the learner's exposure to naturalistic and authentic language and examines gains made in pronunciation accuracy and/or native-like attainment during the SA experience in contrast to students AH or in IM. This research has also focused on acquisition of social and regional variation in the L2, as learners may be exposed to different dialects of the L2 than taught in class, depending on the context of the SA experience and the SNs they develop during the SA. As the key findings, outlined in this section, suggest, it is not the SA itself that is significant but rather what the students *do* during the SA – their level of engagement with the L2 and speakers of L2, underscoring the findings in relation to L2 contact and exposure. Study abroad may benefit both production and perception and may raise awareness of socio-phonetic variation in the L2 as it is one way through which L2 learners are exposed to naturalistic and authentic language, as well as social/regional/ethnic variation in the L2.

5.2 Study Abroad Findings

Research suggests that SA experiences can benefit learners, though there are mitigating factors. The key findings are shown in Table 4 and then discussed in detail.

These findings are discussed here.

- *The SA experience can lead to greater L2 pronunciation gains than AH language learning.*

A robust body of research has found that SA benefits a range of pronunciation domains, including both segmental and suprasegmental features, as well as L2 accent ratings. Gains in consonant and vowel accuracy have been found in research on American students learning L2 Spanish in a Spanish-dominant country. As an example, Lord (2010) found that university students studying L2 Spanish during SA had significant gains in their accuracy of Spanish spirantization, the realization of the voiced stops /b d g/ as the fricatives [β ð ɣ]. Increased accuracy in the production of Spanish voiceless stops and syllable final lateral have also been found for SA compared with AH students receiving Spanish instruction in the classroom (Díaz-Campos, 2006). Nagle, Morales-Front, Moorman, and Sanz (2016) found gains in VOT duration and articulatory accuracy by L1 English L2 Spanish learners during an SA experience in Spain. Stevens (2011) also found that L2 Spanish vowel accuracy improved for SA but not AH students.

SA experiences may also support suprasegmental gains. Trimble (2013) found that learners of Spanish who had an SA experience in Venezuela made gains in L2 Spanish intonation by adopting new patterns for declaratives and absolute interrogatives, increasing their consistency in using new intonation patterns, and by expanding their pitch range. Henriksen, Geeslin, and Willis (2010) found that L1 English learners of L2 Spanish improved their use of pitch accent and final boundary tone movements during SA in Spain.

Table 4 A summary of findings on study abroad and L2 phonetics/phonology

- *The SA experience can lead to greater L2 pronunciation gains than AH language learning.*
- *Younger learners can achieve L2 pronunciation gains during an SA experience.*
- *SA may not only benefit language development – it may increase awareness of dialectal differences and/or other variation in usage of different L2 phonological features which, in turn, may impact dialect preferences.*
- *Not all L2 pronunciation features improve as a result of SA.*
- *Prior instruction on specific features may increase gains on these features during the SA experience.*
- *Prior exposure to a dialect prior to SA may lead to greater adoption of features of that dialect.*
- *Proficiency of the learner may impact the benefit of the SA experience on L2 pronunciation gains.*
- *Degree of integration into the L2 social context and ability to develop social networks impact the level of L2 pronunciation gains during the SA experience.*
- *Cultural sensitivity as well as identity may mitigate effects of SA, creating differential outcomes for students on SA programmes.*
- *Gains made during the SA experience may be retained long term, but only for some features and subject to continued language contact and experience.*
- *Length of the SA may impact the overall benefit of this experience.*

Gains in fluency have also been found: Trenchs-Parera (2009) compared Spanish L1 learners of English in an FI setting in Spain versus English L1 learners of L2 Spanish on an SA experience in Spain. While both the FI and SA learners made fluency gains, the SA students had fewer disruptions and more fluent speech after the SA. Mora and Valls-Ferrer (2012) found robust fluency gains for English L1 Spanish L2 learners during an SA in Spain in comparison to students who only received FI AH. Segalowitz and colleagues (2004), in research on a one-semester AH versus SA American students learning L2 Spanish, found that only the SA students made significant gains on fluency measures, including rate of speech, mean length of utterance without fillers, and length of longest utterance without hesitations or fillers.

In addition, research has found that perceived foreign accent, as assessed by ratings by NS judges, can improve during an SA experience: Martinsen, Alvord, and Tanner (2014) found that students with an extensive SA experience had significantly more native-like accent ratings than students who had AH classroom instruction only. Avello, Mora, and Pérez-Vidal (2012) found a decrease in pronunciation errors as well as a slight, though non-significant, increase in more native-like ratings for L1 English L2 Spanish students after a three-month SA in Spain. Munoz and Llanes (2014) found that the SA experience led to more native-like ratings for both L1 Spanish children and adults learners of English in comparison to children and adults AH.

Other studies, however, have found that the SA experience does not lead to any pronunciation gains or that the SA experience leads to a decrease in pronunciation accuracy. Avello and Lara (2014), for example, did not find significant improvement for VOT measures of /t k/ in initial position or the /iː – ɪ/ *(beat vs. bit)* and /æ – ʌ/ *(bat vs. but)* vowel contrasts from Spanish L1 learners of English. As they note, the lack of segmental development during the SA experience may be due to the stronger focus on communicative ability rather than accuracy, as well as the possibility that the learners discovered that accuracy was not related to intelligibility (e.g., that they did not have to approximate NS models to be understood). It is also likely that the features assessed – English VOT and vowel contrasts – are more difficult to acquire by L1 speakers of Spanish as the differences between English and Spanish for these features may be less salient or noticeable to the learner. As will be discussed in more detail, the features that occur more frequently in the input or are more noticeable to the learner are more likely to benefit from the SA experience. Other factors, including proficiency, prior instruction, and length of the SA may also explain differential results.

- *Younger learners can achieve L2 pronunciation gains during an SA experience.*

While SA research has typically focused on university students, studies that have included children have found that younger learners can make significant L2 pronunciation gains during the SA experience. In research on L1 Spanish-speaking children learning English either AH or during an SA experience in Ireland, Llanes (2016) found that only children who had an SA experience significantly improved their L2 pronunciation, as measured by a foreign-accent rating task. Munoz and Llanes (2014) found that while age (child vs. adult) was not a significant factor in changes in degree of foreign accent, child participants (ages 10–11) had the most significant gains overall and more speaking time with NSs than the adult participants, which may have led to greater L2 gains than those found for adults. As discussed in Section 4, it is likely that younger learners were able to develop the types of L2 contact through peer group friendships that lead to more L2 use opportunities during the SA more easily than adults. Adults, in contrast, may have more difficulty developing social contacts during the SA experience, which may then limit their opportunities to engage in the L2 meaningfully during the SA (see also Ader & Miljan, 2015 and Moyer, 2004, as already discussed). These findings indicate that age may need to be examined as a social variable, a factor that limits or fosters contact with speakers of the L2.

- *SA may not only benefit language development – it may increase awareness of dialectal differences and/or other variation in usage of different L2 phonological features which, in turn, may impact dialect preferences.*

Research suggests that the potential benefits of SA extend beyond linguistic gains to metalinguistic and sociolinguistic knowledge about the L2 which, in turn, may impact L2 acquisition and use. The SA experience may impact attitudes towards different dialects, resulting in the targeting of specific features associated with a given dialect. Ringer-Hilfinger (2012), for example, in work on L2 Spanish acquisition, found that SA participants had greater sociolinguistic awareness of allophonic variation of the voiceless dental fricative /θ/ as [θ], [s], or [z] in Castilian Spanish (as in *[θ]apato, [s]apato,* or *[z]apato* in the word *zapato,* 'shoe') than AH students, and that the SA students had formed opinions about how to use the variants of /θ/. The SA students who had more contact with NSs of Spanish in Madrid and less contact with NSs of Spanish in the United States had the greatest usage of the [θ] variant, a feature of the local dialect in Madrid that is not widely used in the Spanish spoken in the United States.

Schmidt (2020) examined whether L2 learners of Spanish adopted local variants of Argentinian Spanish for /s/, [h] or [s] or deletion (as in *espalda*, 'back', with [h] as in *ehpalda*, [s] as in *espalda*, and deleted, as in *epalda*) as well as the use of [j ʃ ʒ] in words with 'y' or 'll' such as *calle* ('street'), as in [kaje], [kaʃe], or [kaʒe] after an SA experience. Prior contact with speakers of Argentinian Spanish prior to the SA experience was significant, probably because of the exposure to, possible awareness of, and positive attitudes towards these variants established through previous contact with Argentinian Spanish. In addition, some of the SA participants had changed their preference towards Spanish dialects by the end of the SA, from Castilian or Mexican Spanish or no preference, to a preference for an Argentinian dialect. There was a positive correlation between those who had greater usage of the Argentinian variants and a preference for an Argentinian dialect, indicating that the learners' 'accent aims' (see Rindal, 2010) are related to their linguistic choices.

Chappell and Kanwit (2022) examined effect of SA on L2 Spanish learners' identification of social characteristics of Spanish speakers based on their use of one of two variants of /s/, [s] or [h] (as in *esquina*, 'corner', as [eskina] or [ehkina]) and found that awareness of the [h] variant was higher among those who had studied abroad in regions in which this dialectal variant was present. These students had gained knowledge about the social status and function of [h] versus [s], thereby expanding their understanding of the L2. These studies illustrate the importance of SA on the development of L2 socio-phonetic and socio-phonological awareness and competence.

- *Not all L2 pronunciation features improve as a result of SA.*

As discussed in Section 4, there are differential gains in accuracy for pronunciation features during an immersive language experience and/or through high levels of L2 contact and exposure. Greater accuracy in usage appears to occur when learners are aware of the articulation as well as the usage of a given feature, when the feature is more salient to the learner, acoustically or through frequency in the input, or if the learner has received prior instruction on the feature. Some features that are more difficult to acquire may require a longer SA period and/or FI and SA.

Díaz-Campos (2006) found differential results for the improvement of phonological features by AH versus SA American students studying L2 Spanish. While SA students made greater gains on voiceless stops and syllable final laterals, AH students made more improvements on accuracy in production of intervocalic fricatives. In addition, differential results by vowel type have been found: while Stevens (2011) found that American students undergoing an SA experience in Spain showed improvement in L2 Spanish vowel accuracy, not all vowels benefitted equally from the SA experience, with the highest accuracy rates found for /i/ (as in *si*, 'yes') and /u/ (as in *grupo*, 'group'), followed by /o/ (*loco*, 'crazy'), /e/ (as in *bebe*, 'baby'), and least for /a/ (as in *papa*, 'father'). It is likely that some vowels, for instance /i/ and /u/, are more perceptually salient and therefore easier to acquire.

SA gains may predominate for production while AH formal instruction (FI) may lead to greater gains in perception than during SA, as research on the acquisition of English L2 VOT by Spanish L1 learners by Mora (2008) found. Mora (2008) examined both perception and production of VOT duration and found that FI led to significant perception gains while SA led to production gains.

Oral proficiency and fluency, in particular, may benefit from the SA experience. Mora and Valls-Ferrer (2012) examined the development of oral fluency, accuracy, and complexity of AH and SA for EFL learners in Spain (AH) and L1 speakers of English learning L2 Spanish during an SA experience. While the AH students did not have any gains, the gains of the SA were highest on oral fluency, followed by accuracy, with few to no gains on complexity during SA. Segalowitz and colleagues (2004) found that SA L2 Spanish learners from the

United States made significant gains for oral proficiency and fluency in contrast to the AH group. However, the SA group did not have gains in grammatical abilities in contrast to the AH group. In a study on L2 learners of English in Spanish (FI) and L2 learners of Spanish on an SA programme in Spain, Mora and Valls-Ferrer (2012) found that SA learners made gains on fluency, with some accuracy gains but no gains on complexity. The FI group did not make significant gains on any of the measures. Comparing the oral fluency development of students in AH, IM, and SA French L2 programmes, Freed, Segalowitz, and Dewey (2004) found that while the AH group made no gains, the SA group made significant gains in one oral fluency measure, speech fluidity. The IM group, however, made the greatest gains, and had gains across a number of measures: total number of words spoken, length of longest turn, rate of speech, and speech fluidity. The researchers note that the IM students had significantly more speaking and writing in French than the AH or SA groups while the SA group used more of the L1 than the IM group, underscoring the importance not only of exposure to the L2 but how the learners engage with the L2, and the benefits of sustained contact with the L2 through diverse modes on L2 pronunciation attainment (see Section 4;and Moyer, 2011).

In addition, language gains may be more evident if assessment is conducted through more conversational tasks, as research by Díaz-Campos (2006) found: SA students had higher accurate rates for initial stops, syllable-final laterals and palatal nasals than FI students when assessed through a conversation rather than a reading-aloud task, probably due to the prevalence of conversational speech styles during the SA experience.

These findings indicate that some aspects of L2 development, and particularly oral communication skills, benefit more from an SA experience, whereas discrete language elements, such as grammatical features, may benefit less from SA and more from a classroom instruction setting. In addition, how the learners engage with the L2, and the L1, during the SA, directly impacts the benefits of the SA experience, as does how gains are assessed.

- *Prior instruction on specific features may increase gains on these features during the SA experience.*

Research suggests that gains on some L2 features may be enhanced if there is a FI component prior to the SA or IM experience, likely due to the raised awareness developed by learners of the use and articulation of these features through FI. Lord (2010), for example, found that while all students made gains in the accuracy of L2 Spanish spirantization of the voiced stops /b d g/ to [β ð ɣ] during an IM experience, the students who had prior pronunciation instruction made the greatest gains, leading the researcher to argue that a combination of both pronunciation instruction and immersion/SA was more beneficial than either immersion or instruction alone. Research by Mora (2008) on the acquisition of VOT duration for English L2 learners with Spanish L1 suggests that FI before SA fosters L2 gains. Mora examined both perception and production of VOT duration and found that while FI led to significant perception gains, SA led to production gains, possibly due to the preceding instruction on VOT during the FI prior to the SA experience.

Conversely, research has suggested that less L2 instruction may help acquisition: Alvord and Christensen (2012) found that English L1 Spanish L2 adult students who had less FI prior to the SA experience made the greatest gains on voiced approximants. This is possibly because learners with more prior instruction may have more to 'unlearn', especially if what is taught in the classroom is more formal or focuses on standard models/features that are less widely used in a specific L2 context. In addition, as discussed in Sections 3 and 4, learners may target non-standard or regional features when immersed in the L2 setting; assessment of segmental gains during SA that is based on standard models of the L2 may inadvertently overlook socio-phonetic gains made by learners during the L2 and/or assess the L2 features that the learners acquired during the SA as 'incorrect' or 'non-standard' in comparison to the models taught and assessed AH in the L2 classroom.

- *Prior exposure to a dialect prior to SA may lead to greater adoption of features of that dialect.*

Exposure to an L2, a particular variety or dialect of the L2, and features of the L2 prior to the SA experience appears to benefit L2 pronunciation gains as well as adoption of features of a given dialect. Schmidt (2020), for example, found that SA students who had contact with speakers of Argentinian Spanish prior to their SA experience in Buenos Aries had greater adoption of features of this variety of Spanish during the SA. One reason for this is that the SA students with previous contact with the dialect may have had greater awareness of the dialectal use of the features under study (for examples the allophones of /s/) in Argentinian Spanish, and therefore more likely to notice – and use – these features when in Argentina. Another reason is that these features would be more attractive to the participants with prior contact with speakers of Argentinian Spanish, due to friendships with users of these features in their home country.

- *Proficiency of the learner may impact the benefit of the SA experience on L2 pronunciation gains.*

Pre-SA programme proficiency has received attention, with research suggesting benefits for students at both higher and lower proficiency. Bejarano and colleagues (2019), for example, found that L2 English learners with higher oral proficiency made greater fluency gains during the SA, though the size of the students' SNs (see Section 3) significantly impacted gains. Kennedy Terry (2022) found that students with a higher pre-departure proficiency made greater oral fluency gains during the SA experience. Baker-Smemoe and colleagues (2014), in contrast, found that the students with lower proficiency on SA programmes in L2 Chinese, French, Russian, and Arabic made greater gains as measured by oral proficiency tests than students with higher levels of proficiency. Casillas (2020) found that absolute beginners in a seven-week domestic immersion programme on L2 Spanish made significant gains on VOT for voiced stops, with significant gains occurring around twenty-one days into the immersion. Fewer changes were found for VOT for voiceless stops, indicating that gains are variable, and that some features are more likely to improve early in the L2 acquisition process.

It is possible that a higher proficiency is necessary for learners to gain awareness of the articulation and use of certain features, particularly those which are more difficult or less frequent or salient in the input and/or features in variation in the L2 context. The beneficial effect of previous instruction on L2 pronunciation gains during the SA experience is likely due to an increased proficiency. Other features, particularly those that are more salient or easy to acquire, may benefit from SA for learners even at a lower proficiency level.

- *Degree of integration into the L2 social context and ability to develop social networks impact the level of L2 pronunciation gains during the SA experience.*

Given the findings discussed in Sections 3 and 4, it is perhaps not surprising that findings from SA research indicate that an important factor in the achievement of L2 pronunciation gains during SA is contact with the L2 as well as development of SNs during the SA.

Stevens (2011), for example, found that exposure to Spanish television during the SA experience was a significant factor in Spanish L2 vowel gains by American students, with higher rates of TV exposure linked to higher vowel accuracy rates, possibly due to the increased L2 input the learners were exposed to through TV. In addition, SA students with less use of their L1 (English) made greater gains on Spanish vowels than those who used more English during the SA experience. Trimble (2013), in research on suprasegmental gains by L2 learners of Spanish on an SA experience in Venezuela, found that the SA students who spoke more Spanish and less English (their L1) had greater suprasegmental gains than those who spoke less Spanish and more English. Munoz and Llanes (2014), in research on child and adult Spanish L1 English L2 students in AH versus SA, found that gains in the L2 during the SA were significantly correlated with hours speaking English, hours speaking with NSs, and hours in class.

The ability to establish viable SNs as well as the size and density of these networks (see Section 3), impacts L2 pronunciation gains during the SA. Müller (2016), for example, found that L1 English L2 German students who were able to develop viable L2 SNs made greater L2 pronunciation gains during the SA compared with students who did not develop viable L2 SNs. Kennedy Terry (2017) found that SNs with NSs were a significant predictor of acquisition of target-like sociolinguistic variation in French by L1 speakers of English during their SA. Kennedy Terry (2022), in similar research, found that the only extralinguistic predictor of deletion of /l/, a variable feature of French, by American students on an SA experience in France, was size and density of SNs, with larger and more dense networks a predictor of more target-like /l/ deletion patterns.

As these findings show, immersion in an L2 environment is not sufficient in itself for L2 gains. Both what the learners do in the L2 and with whom they use the L2 significantly impact what they target for acquisition and use and their overall L2 pronunciation gains.

- *Cultural sensitivity as well as identity may the mitigate effects of SA, creating differential outcomes for students on an SA programme.*

Research indicates that not all students benefit equally from the SA experience. Other factors may impact the students' L2 pronunciation gains during the IM or SA experience. Several studies (Baker-Smemoe et al., 2014; Martinsen, 2008) on American students on an SA in Spain found that higher levels of intercultural sensitivity, and the ability to be open to and accepting of cultural differences, pre-departure of the SA, was associated with gains in L2 Spanish oral proficiency development and/or L2 pronunciation accuracy during the SA.

Other factors may play a role as well: Müller (2016) found that learners' beliefs about the importance of accurate or native-like pronunciation in the L2, participation in the local community, as well as perceived obstacles to learning, could explain varying outcomes among Canadian students learning L2 German on an SA experience in Germany. Students who believed that L2 learners should strive towards a more native-like pronunciation may position themselves as inferior to NSs, thus creating difficulties for them to develop a viable L2 identity (see also Section 7), and be less likely to use the L2. Students who orient towards intelligibility rather than native-like accuracy may be less inhibited in L2 use during the SA experience as they are able to construct a viable L2 identity. Students who are able to construct a viable identity may have greater L2 gains during the SA.

The context of the SA experience may also impact outcomes: findings by Baker-Smemoe and colleagues (2014) on 102 students from the United States on SA programmes for Spanish, Chinese, French, Russian, and Arabic found that while 60 per cent of the SA students made oral language gains, the China programme saw the highest percentage of gains across students, with 80 per cent of these SA students making gains. In contrast, students in an SA experience in France had the lowest overall gains, with only 40 per cent of students making oral proficiency gains.

As these studies suggest, several factors – including the context of the SA itself and learners' beliefs about L2 learning and their cross-cultural sensitivity – can impact SA outcomes. These factors require further exploration as they offer some insight into the sometimes conflicting results of SA research.

- *Gains made during the SA experience may be retained long term, but only for some features and subject to continued language contact and experience.*

The long-term benefits of SA need further investigation. The limited research to date indicates that some aspects of L2 pronunciation gains may be retained long-term, but that L2 contact and use are important components in retention. Huensch, Tracy-Ventura, Bridges, and Cuesta Medina (2019) investigated the maintenance and attrition of L2 oral proficiency by L2 Spanish and L2 French students four years after their SA experience. The researchers found that speech rate, which improved significantly during SA, was retained four years later, but the maintenance of oral proficiency was greatest for the students who were categorized as having more intense L2 exposure in the four years after the SA experience.

- *Length of the SA may impact the overall benefit of this experience.*

As the research discussed previously illustrates, the IM or SA experience can last from several weeks to a semester or even a year or two. Most commonly, research has focused on one-semester SA experiences as these are more typical in university language programmes, the research context of many of the studies on SA. While a shorter SA may have benefits, particularly for aspects of oral fluency including speech rate, other aspects of the L2, including sociolinguistic variation, less salient, less frequent, and more difficult features, may not benefit from a shorter SA experience.

Several studies have examined the length of the SA experience. Højen (2003) found that his participants made significant improvements on the foreign accent ratings during the SA, with a longer SA (up to eleven months) leading to a less accented speech rating. Kennedy Terry (2022) examined the acquisition of French sociolinguistic variation patterns by American students on an SA in France over one semester versus one year and found that students on the one-year SA had more target-like /l/ (as in *elle m'a dit* ('she told me') as [ɛl̠ ma di] or with /l/ elision as [ɛ ma di]) and schwa deletion patterns than the students on the one-term SA, though both groups made gains.

A lack of improvement for some features have been found for shorter SA (six months or less). Shively (2008), for example, suggests that the lack of improvement in spirantization among SA students studying L2 Spanish in Spain was due to the shorter SA period between one and six months, and that a longer SA period would lead to greater accuracy for this L2 feature. Comparing the acquisition of English VOT and patterns and vowel duration contrasts by Spanish L1 speakers during a three-month versus a six-month SA, Avello and Lara (2014) did not find significant gains for either the shorter or the longer SA students. It is probable that both VOT and vowel duration contrasts are more difficult to acquire and may require a long SA and/or a combination of pre-departure FI and SA.

Research suggests that longer SA or IM experiences may yield more benefits, not only due to greater exposure to the L2, but also because students in longer SA programmes may be more motivated to develop SNs with target-language speakers than students who are only in the L2 context for a more limited amount of time. This may help explain the differential outcomes in findings on SA discussed previously.

In sum, the robust body of SA research suggests that SA has benefits across a range of L2 pronunciation domains including both segmental and suprasegmental features and oral fluency. Study abroad is also an important means through which L2 learners are exposed to socio-phonetic and dialectal variation in the L2, enabling them to expand their L2 competence beyond standard models taught in the L2 classroom. What the students do in and with the L2 during the SA is crucial to L2 pronunciation gains, and engaging with target speakers of the L2 and with the L2 across diverse modes fosters L2 pronunciation gains. Study abroad may also increase learners' awareness of dialectal variation in the L2, which may influence their own accent aims. As a result, students may return from the SA experience using L2 features that are not as widely used or taught in their home L2 classroom. Rather than being viewed negatively as incorrect or non-standard features, the use of regional variants by L2 learners should be perceived as indicative of increased socio-phonetic competence in the L2. Gender may also impact how learners engage with the L2 and their L2 use opportunities; this is explored in Section 6.

6 Gender

6.1 Defining Gender

Research on gender differences in L2 learning and, in particular, L2 pronunciation attainment, has been a focus of L2 acquisition research since the 1960s.

Early research conceptualized gender as a biological construct, with the sex of the participants a predictor variable for pronunciation accuracy (for a review of this line of research, see, for example, Piske, MacKay, and Flege, 2001). Despite mixed results, the misattribution to biology has persisted. In a recent review of this research, Hansen Edwards, Chan, Lam, and Wang (2021) argue:

> It is our belief that the studies (see Piske et al., 2001, for a review) which have concluded that biological differences explain any gender differences in pronunciation accuracy are flawed in assuming that this equates to a language learning advantage for females, when it may instead be due to a gender-based difference in what is targeted for pronunciation. We believe that while differences in biological sex do not lead to innate differences in the ability to acquire an L2, social differences related to gender may impact L2 pronunciation attainment. (p. 38)

A better way of conceptualizing gender is to view it as 'something individuals do as opposed to something individuals are or have' (Ehrlich, 1997, p. 422). Gender is a significant factor in L2 acquisition and use of phonetic and phonological features, not because girls/women are inherently predisposed to be better at learning language, but because opportunities, access, and peer group networks may differ between genders due to L1 and/or L2 cultural norms. It may be the case, as Moyer (2016) states, that girls/women develop more positive self-concepts as L2 learners due to gender-differential attitudes for language learning that persist. Teacher ideologies and the pervasive myth that girls tend to do better than boys in language acquisition may impact both girls' and boys' self-concepts. As a result, girls may outperform boys in part because they are told they are better language learners, and internalizing this ideology may lead to higher motivation to study the L2 (see Moyer, 2016).

The results of L2 as well as sociolinguistic research on gender and language acquisition and use has found that gender differences exist for some learners in not only what of the L2 is acquired but also in how the L2 is used. It is important to note, however, that this research examines these differences in gender differences in speech communities, peer groups, opportunities and access, and not biological differences that impact cognitive abilities to learn an L2.

6.2 Gender Findings

The current review of research on gender views gender as a social construct, and examines how gender fosters or limits access to L1 and L2 use opportunities as well as local speech norms in the L2, if gender differences exist for these norms. A key summary of findings is presented in Table 5.

These findings are discussed below.

Table 5 A summary of key findings on gender and L2 phonetics and phonology

- *Learners acquire not only the L2, but also (gendered) sociolinguistic patterns that exist in the local community.*
- *Women may be language innovators in the L2, with greater use of supralocal variants or leading the usage of new L2 variants.*
- *Historical factors may impact the social networks women/men develop and the diversity of their social networks which, in turn, may impact their dialect repertoire.*
- *Gender and peer social networks are often intertwined; what may be interpreted as gender-based differences can be due to use of features associated with a particular peer network.*
- *L1 cultural norms may influence the access L2 speakers have to L2 acquisition and use opportunities.*
- *Conflicts may exist between L2 gendered speech norms and the learners' L1 identity, resulting in resistance and/or avoidance of some L2 features.*

- *Learners acquire not only the L2, but also (gendered) sociolinguistic patterns that exist in the local community.*

L2 learners may be aware of gender differences in the use of different variants in the L2. In a perception study, Solon and Kanwit (2022) examined the preference of L2 learners of Spanish for a realized or deleted intervocalic /d/, which is variably realized in Spanish as an approximant (as in *canta<u>d</u>o*, 'sung', as [kantá<u>ð</u>o], or deleted, as in [kantáo]), and whether gender of the speaker was a factor in the learners' preferences for the realized or deleted /d/. They found a gender preference for deletion, with men favoring deletion, a pattern that aligns with findings from research on /d/ deletion by NSs of Spanish. The linguistic constraints that the learners' favoured for /d/ deletion – including grammatical constraints and preceding vowels – replicated those found for NSs of Spanish. This indicates that learners had already internalized gender variation patterns as well as the sociolinguistic constraints on /d/ deletion. These findings were consistent across all proficiency levels, including students with lower levels of Spanish ability, indicating that gendered sociolinguistic variation patterns may be acquired in the early stages of language development.

Research (see, for example, Coates & Pichler, 2011; Eckert & McConnell-Ginet, 1999) suggests that L1 women are more likely to use standard or prestige variants whereas men may use more non-standard features. These differences probably exist due the advantages that standard speech may confer to women in terms of educational, social, and economic access. L2 research suggests that not only are L2 learners aware of gender differences that may exist in the local community, but that they target the gendered speech norms that exist among NSs of the target language – in other words, L2 learners linguistically accommodate to the gendered speech norms of target-language speakers. Adamson and Regan (1991), for example, in research on Cambodian and Vietnamese immigrants to the United States, found the learners targeted the local speech norms for (ing) variation, with the women using the standard variant [iŋ] (*swimming*) while men used the non-standard variant [ɪn] (*swimmin'*), replicating the local gender norms for (ing) variation for NSs. Research by Díaz-Campos (2004) found that for L2 learners of Spanish (L1 English), gender differences in pronunciation norms existed, with women favouring a more native-like pronunciation and the men disfavouring a native-like pronunciation. Chan's (2018) research on attitudes towards different varieties of English by secondary school students in Hong Kong found that gender differences existed, with girls favouring an NS accent, adopting this as their educational model and 'accent aim'. In contrast, boys had a greater acceptance of a local Hong Kong English accent. Work by Hiang and Gupta (1992) on the use of postvocalic /r/ (*car, farm*) in SgE (see also Section 4), found a greater use of /r/ among university women than university men. They argue that /r/ is a prestige variable in SgE, and that this may explain higher rates of usage among women. Expanding on the research on /r/ in SgE, Kwek and Low (2021) examined the use of a labiodental approximant variant of /r/ as [ʋ] (as in *really* as *[ʋ]eally*) in place of or together with the more common realization as a post-alveolar approximant [ɹ] (*really* as *[ɹ]eally*), among Chinese Singaporean university students or graduates. They found a significantly higher usage of the labiodental approximant for women than men across different speech tasks, including conversational data and read speech (short passage, sentences, and word list). They concluded that the labiodental approximant variant is a characteristic of young educated female SgE speech. While the authors do not offer an explanation for the gender differences found in the use of this variant, they do note that it is perceived to be 'effeminate' in BrE. It is possible that this social meaning is spreading into SgE as well, leading and/or fostered by a higher usage of the variant among women in Singapore.

Research by Habib (2014) on the use of the vowels in rural versus urban dialects in Syria found different patterns of usage by gender and age: younger children had the lowest rates of usage of the rural vowels, with greater use among older children. Among the older children, there was greater use of the rural vowels by boys over girls, possibly due to the boys' desire to assert a local – and more masculine – identity, as the use of the rural vowels is more common among adult men than adult women. In contrast, the girls targeted the urban variants, in line with the more common usage of the urban vowels by women than men. As Habib notes, these different linguistic choices are likely due to cultural differences in gender roles in Syria, with men expected to stay close to their parents, often remaining in the local rural villages, whereas women would move to live with their husband's family upon marriage, usually leaving the local community. Consequently, boys may be more likely to acquire the local dialect features than girls. This pattern is well established by L1 sociolinguistic variationist research – boys/men use more non-standard and/or local features than girls/women (see, for example, Trudgill, 2001). More recent research, as discussed earlier, underscores this finding and extends it to multilingual and multidialectal speakers of English as well as less studied languages.

The differential uses of features may support the myth that women are better at learning languages if they use more standard – and thus more 'accurate' – features of the L2, though as some of the research discussed illustrates, cultural differences may explain the differential 'accent aims' and L2 pronunciation outcomes by girls/women and boys/men.

- *Women may be language innovators in the L2, with greater use of supralocal variants or leading the usage of new L2 variants.*

Research suggests that women may be language innovators, more likely to target or use new variants and lead linguistic change (see also Labov, 1990). This has been found for both women using their L1 and in L2 acquisition of phonological features, and across a range of phonological features.

In Manchester, England, as an example, Polish L1 women immigrants may be helping to lead linguistic change for T Glottaling. Drummond (2011) examined the use of T Glottalling by immigrants from Poland who had moved to Manchester as adults. T Glottalling is the realization of the /t/ in word-medial (*bottle*) or word-final environments (*lit*) as a glottal stop (this sounds like a quick 'uh'). It occurs frequently in word-final position in many varieties of English, and less often in word-medial position, though this latter usage is spreading across England. It is considered a supralocal variable, which is a term to denote a linguistic variable that has wider regional usage and is adopted more widely than local variants. Drummond found gender differences in the use of T Glottalling, with greater usage by women than men. He argues that women are more likely to acquire supralocal patterns of NSs whereas men are more likely to acquire more local features. This could be because women are more likely to accommodate their speech to others and tend to have wider social networks or greater contact with a range of people in some contexts (see Sharma, 2011). Drummond argues that this is because gender norms in the L1 community may impact the occupations to which L2 learners are able to gain access in a given context. In Manchester, for example, the women in the study were more likely to find positions in a department store, bar, office, restaurant, or as a university researcher, while the men found jobs in a factory or as a mechanic. Similar gendered professions were reported by Hansen Edwards (2009).

GOOSE-fronting, also a supralocal variable, has been associated with Polish L1 teen girls in Manchester. In research on adolescent Roma migrants, Howley (2015) found that the teen girls had significantly more GOOSE-fronting than boys. GOOSE-fronting is the realization of the GOOSE vowel, a high back rounded vowel, with a more centralized articulation. GOOSE-fronting is a supralocal variable that is spreading across the United Kingdom and United States. Howley found differences in GOOSE-fronting among the adolescent girls based on peer group networks, with more fronting among the girls with stronger non-Roma than Roma networks. The girls with the most non-Roma friendships had higher rates of GOOSE-fronting than their Manchester peers, indicating that they were hypercorrecting (overusing GOOSE-fronting in the belief that this usage is standard among local peers), possibly due to their awareness about and targeting of the local speech norms for this feature.

Women may also be leading the fronting of FOOT as well as DH-stopping in London: In research on MLE, a variety of BrE spoken in multi-ethnic areas of London, Cheshire, Kerswill, Fox, and Torgersen (2011) found that women (both Anglos and non-Anglos) were leading in the fronting of FOOT, a linguistic change occurring in varieties of BrE, though it is not as prevalent as GOOSE-fronting. Women were also more likely to have DH-stopping (the realization of the voiced dental fricative /ð/ as [d]) than men, with higher usage among non-Anglo women over Anglo women. DH-stopping is also a supralocal feature that is spreading across Englishes globally. These studies highlight the importance of considering gender as a social construct and gendered sociolinguistic variation patterns in the L1/L2 community when examining the acquisition of L2 pronunciation, as use of particular L2 features (such as T Glottaling or DH-stopping) may not be due to lack of ability to acquire particular L2 features but rather the targeting of gendered speech norms that exist in the social groups to which people have access.

- *Historical factors may impact the social networks women/men develop and the diversity of their social networks which, in turn, may impact their dialect repertoire.*

As discussed in Section 3, Sharma's (2011) research on Punjab Indians in Southall, London found that older men and younger women had more style shifting in the use of the retroflex [ʈ] than [t̪] (as in *t̪an)* than younger men and older women, due to the more diverse social networks that both older men and younger women developed, in contrast to younger men and older women. Sharma posited that historical factors may impact the diversity of SNs that younger and older men and women develop which, in turn, impacts the linguistic repertoires they develop as a result of the diversity of their networks. Both older men, growing up as minority group members who needed to establish British networks for employment, and younger women, seeking to advance their own educational and occupational opportunities, had larger SNs outside the family and greater exposure to the British community. Older women had more home or family ties while younger men had more local employment and local friendship networks. As a result, older men and younger women had greater exposure to other varieties of BrE, and an expanded linguistic repertoire in comparison with older women and younger men, who had primarily IndE or British Asian networks and linguistic repertoires. As discussed, age may also be a factor in the development of L2 social networks, and may interact with gender, as Sharma's research suggests, given that older women had limited access to SNs outside the immediate family or home, due to historical gender roles.

- *Gender and peer social networks are often intertwined: what may be interpreted as gender-based differences can be due to use of features associated with a particular peer network.*

Gender and peer group networks are often inter-related, and differences in the use of linguistic variants that are interpreted as gender differences may in fact be due to use of particular features in a peer group network that is same sex. In other words, it may be difficult to extrapolate gender from peer group networks (see Section 3). Research by Meyerhoff and Schleef (2012) on the use of the variants of (ing) (*swimming*) by Polish L1 teenagers in London and Edinburgh found that gender was significant among the London teenagers, with Polish boys in London more likely to use the standard variant, the velar [ɪŋ] (*swimming*), than girls, who were more likely to use the local variant [ɪn] (*swimmin'*). This pattern was different than that found for NS teens in London, as the NS boys were more likely to use the local variant while girls were more likely to use the standard variant. In Edinburgh, gender was not significant, though friendship group networks were significant, with Polish teens in Edinburgh with mostly Polish peer networks more likely to use the velar [ɪŋ] than those with mixed Scottish-Polish networks, who were more likely to use the local variant [ɪn]. Meyerhoff and Schleef argued that the differential gender patterns found in London could be because L2 learners may establish social distinctions in L2 use that are not found among NSs. As they state,

> Since among teenagers, gender and friendship networks are not unrelated (teenagers tend to hang out with same sex peers, see Cameron [2005, p. 28]

> for a review of studies showing this), we would like to suggest that the gender effects in London and the friendship network effects in Edinburgh are perhaps different facets of the same processes of translating variation into sociolinguistically meaningful patterns. (p. 407)

They further argue that since gender is a social category that attracts more attention (e.g., it is more salient) than others, as are peer networks, with the latter often influenced by gender, the Polish L1 learners of English are acquiring the linguistic patterns found in their community and are replicating the patterns found among their friends, who may be same sex. In other words, in the London community, the Polish L1 learners may be targeting the (ing) variation patterns found among same-sex peers, who probably comprise their friendship networks. Similarly, the Polish teens in Edinburgh target the L2 use patterns found among their peer networks, which may be comprised of same-sex peers.

- *L1 and/or L2 cultural norms may influence the access L2 speakers have to L2 acquisition and use opportunities.*

Cultural norms in the L1 and the L2 community can act as a barrier or create access to L1/L2 use opportunities, which may result in differential targets for acquisition outcomes. In my research (Hansen Edwards, 2009) on a husband and wife, both immigrants from Vietnam living in the south-western region of the United States, I found that L1 gender roles for occupational attainment led to differential L2 pronunciation attainment. I found that the wife had limited L2 use opportunities due to her career pathway as a nail technician, an occupation that was easily accessible to female immigrants from Vietnam in the city in which they lived in the United States. While her occupation meant she interacted with non-Vietnamese speaking customers during her workday, her interactions were relatively superficial and she relied on formulaic questions to engage her clients. Her husband found work in a more male-dominant profession, as a stock filler in a factory. His workmates were from the United States and Mexico and, as a result, he engaged in English interactions with them, particularly during lunch and other breaks. While the wife and husband had similar L2 pronunciation attainment at the beginning of the research, after one year, the husband had greater improvement in consonant accuracy, likely due to his more expansive L2 use opportunities. In his research on Polish L1 immigrants to Manchester, Drummond (2011) also found that the access that the immigrants had to occupations was gendered, which, in term, impacted the exposure the women and men had to the L2 and, importantly, phonological features of the L2. As the women in Drummond's study were more likely to develop wider social networks through their occupational opportunities and accommodate to the speech of these networks, they used more supralocal variants than the immigrant men. Sharma (2011) also found that the Punjab Indian younger women of her study also had wider SNs than younger men and older women through occupational and educational opportunities and, as a result, targeted the variants in wider usage among their social groups.

Gendered norms in the L2 and L1 cultures may also impact overall L2 pronunciation attainment and fluency gains. In research on L1 Kurdish immigrants to Turkey, Polat and Mahalingappa (2010) found that more Turkish native-like accent ratings among L1 Kurdish girls in contrast to boys could be due to stronger identification with the L2 community the girls had, because of greater socialization with same-gender networks arising from L1 cultural norms, leading to a larger L2 Turkish-speaking network than the boys. The boys, on the other hand, had greater identification with the L1 community, and more interactions within the Kurdish L1 community. As the authors suggest, it is likely that the girls were motivated to develop stronger L2 networks in order to have greater access to educational, and thus occupational, advancement. As the girls had more restrictions on the development of mixed-sex networks than the boys due to L1 Kurdish cultural norms, the same-sex networks they developed included members of the L1 community as well as the L2 community.

Alfayez and Hüttner (2019) conducted research on Saudi Arabian women during an SA experience in the United States and on how the L1 cultural requirement that women must have a male guardian with them to the United States impacted the women's access to L2 social networks and use opportunities during the SA. Gender impacted the SA experience in numerous ways. Initially, some students who had the grade point average required to join the SA were unable to go due to family objections or lack of a male guardian to travel with the student. The second way in which gender impacted the SA experience was that the women were unable to establish many new L2 social networks, instead relying on their assigned target-language 'buddies' (assigned by the host university) or the assigned buddies of their Saudi Arabian peers. These buddy networks enabled the women to engage in L2 use and achieve L2 fluency gains during the SA experience.

These studies suggest that L1/L2 cultural norms may result in women developing larger and more diverse SNs within the L2 community, which, in turn, impacts not only what the women are exposed to of the L2 but also the linguistic expectations on the women (e.g., that they use particular features of the L2 in order to accommodate to the expected speech norms necessary for occupational and educational advancement and success). Differences in the outcomes of L2 acquisition and in the use of particular features of the L2 by women and men are therefore not due to innate biological differences (and an innate advantage for women in language learning) but rather to socially constructed differences in L2 access and use.

- *Conflicts may exist between L2 gendered speech norms and the learners' L1 identity, resulting in resistance and/or avoidance of some L2 features.*

Research has shown that women may avoid using some L2 speech forms if they perceive that these project an image or identity that is at odds with their L1 identity. Both Siegal (1996) and Ohara (2001) researched the acquisition of L2 Japanese by western women and their avoidance of the use of highly gendered features (particle markers in Siegal, 1996 and a high pitch in Ohara, 2001) when speaking Japanese, despite knowing that these features were sociolinguistically appropriate in a given context. As a result, the women may appear to sound 'inaccurate' and/or lacking sociolinguistic awareness when in fact they had both acquired the use of the features and the sociolinguistic knowledge of when and how they should be used, preferring to sound 'inappropriate' or 'inaccurate' rather than projecting a humble or cute feminine image in the L2 at odds with their L1 self-identity.

Gender plays an important role in L2 acquisition not because women or girls are innately better at learning languages than men or boys. Rather, gendered expectations that girls/women are better language learners, their exposure to more linguistic diversity in the L2, and their desire to accommodate to supralocal or more standard speech norms in order to increase their access to occupational and educational opportunities help explain why girls/women may have more standard or native-like L2 pronunciation than men. In sum, gender does not confer biological advantages for girls/women in L2 acquisition; rather, L1 and L2 cultural norms may result in differential L2 access and use opportunities for girls/women in comparison to boys/men, which then results in differences in L2 pronunciation outcomes. Gender is one part of a learner's identity; the following section on identity and ethnic group affiliation examines the influence of cultural and ethnic identity on L2 pronunciation outcomes.

7 Identity and Ethnic Group Affiliation

7.1 Defining Identity and Ethnic Group Affiliation

The last social factors discussed in this Element are identity and ethnic group affiliation. They are discussed together in this section as ethnic group affiliation, or EGA, can be viewed as one dimension of identity – how one's ethnicity impacts one's view of the L1 and L2 language, culture, and speakers. Block (2007, p. 27) defines identities as 'socially constructed, self-conscious, ongoing narratives that individuals perform, interpret and project in dress, bodily movements, actions and language'. Identity can encompass a range of factors, including gender and social and peer group networks, both discussed earlier. Language – and accent – are important dimensions of L1 and L2 identity. Le Page and Tabouret-Keller (1985) state that our language choices are 'acts of identity' that display our group memberships at any given time.

Identity research has been informed by both sociolinguistic and social constructivist frameworks. Sociolinguistic frameworks have been employed in studies (e.g., Lybeck, 2002; Thompson, 1991) that have primarily focused on the acquisition and use of particular phonetic and phonological features and their variants to mark an L1 and/or L2 identity. Research under the social constructivist framework (see Marx, 2002 and Moyer, 2004, as well as Ohara, 2001, in Section 6) has examined how a viable identity in the L2 is constructed – identities are not projected but negotiated. In order to successfully develop a viable L2 identity, the L2 community has to accept the learner's membership into that group. The learner's accent – and whether the learner 'sounds' like a member of a given community (see 'passing' in Section 7.2) – is a key dimension of that acceptance. It is important to note that identities are by nature fluid and, as research has shown (see, for example, Clark, 2007), individuals may alter their pronunciation based on their interactants – accommodating to the speech of their interlocutor to be perceived as belonging to the same group. Learners may move between different pronunciations – using different L1 and L2 features – based on the community or social group with whom they are interacting (Jenkins, 2000). Motivation, and willingness to communicate in the L2, may impact the construction of an L2 identity, as may language attitudes (see Section 2). Pronunciation features offer an important means of marking one's social identity and/or social/peer group memberships, as discussed. L2 learners may resist or avoid usage of L1/L2 phonetic and phonological features in order to project or enact a particular L1 or L2 identity. In addition, L2 learners may use features of the L1 and/or L2 as social marking to signal their L1/L2 membership or ethnic identity.

7.2 Identity and Ethnic Group Affiliation Findings

In the following sections, the discussion of Identity and EGA focuses on how L2 speakers view themselves in relation to and as members of their L1 and L2 communities, and how this informs their linguistic choices in the L1 and/or L2. As the focus of this line of research is the learners' relationship with the L1 and/or L2 community and culture, this research is referred to as cultural identity research. In addition, the discussion focuses on the use of L1 versus L2

Table 6 A summary of key findings on identity and ethnic group affiliation and L2 phonetics and phonology

- *Stronger identification with the L2 community may lead to greater L2 pronunciation attainment or use of L2 features associated with the L2 community.*
- *Learners may resist use of some L2 features in order to retain an L1 identity.*
- *Pronunciation features – in contrast to other linguistic features such as syntactic features – may be more salient markers of a particular identity.*
- *The readiness and/or ability to adopt a secondary identity (an L2 identity not in conflict with L1 identity) may be correlated with higher L2 pronunciation attainment and may be more common in settings where learners do not see a conflict or relationship between identity and accent.*
- *Speakers may construct a 'new' L2 or ethnic identity through the use of unique linguistic features.*
- *Stronger identification with the L2 community may lead to greater L2 pronunciation attainment or use of L2 features associated with the L2 community.*

features to mark EGA, a focus on ethnic identity. Table 6 provides a summary of key findings in these areas.

These findings are discussed here.

- *Stronger identification with the L2 community may lead to greater L2 pronunciation attainment or use of L2 features associated with the L2 community.*

The ability to acculturate to the L2 community and develop a viable L2 identity by learners living in the target language culture is associated with higher levels of L2 pronunciation attainment. As an example, Lybeck (2002) found that a stronger level of acculturation with the Norwegian L2 community, fostered through the development of stronger SNs, was associated with higher levels of usage of the Norwegian pronunciation of /r/, in contrast to the AmE pronunciation of /r/, as well a more target-like pronunciation of Norwegian, for American women living in Norway. In research on immigrants to the United States from a range of ethnic and linguistic backgrounds, Gluszek, Newheiser, and Dovidio (2011) found that identification with American culture was a predictor of judges' ratings of the participants' accents, with those with a stronger identification with American culture rated as having a more native-like pronunciation. Sharma (2005; see Section 2), in research on IndE speakers in the United States, found that some speakers adopted more AmE features. The speakers of IndE who had greater use of the AmE variants expressed a greater interest in accommodating to American culture and projecting a new dialect identity in the United States.

Polat and Schallert (2013) researched the L2 pronunciation attainment of Kurdish L1 immigrants to Turkey and found that the learners who had a stronger identification with the L2 Turkish community or were able to retain a strong L1 identity while developing a strong identity with the L2 community had higher L2 Turkish pronunciation attainment than the learners who had stronger identification with only their L1 community. A key finding from this study is that a strong identification with one community does not exclude strong identification with another. As noted, identity is not static and some learners may be able to develop viable L2 identities while retaining a strong L1 identity, using different L1/L2 features in different contexts to mark their belonging to L1 and L2 groups.

Another line of L2 identity research has focused on *passing* – the ability to use features of the L2 to successfully be viewed as a NS of the L2 by members of the L2 group. Marx (2002) conducted a first-person study on her own experiences as a Canadian L1 speaker of English during her three years in Germany. When she first moved to Germany, her German had a Canadian accent, leading others to perceive her as American, an identity she sought to reject. As a result, she avoided speakers of the L1, working hard to attain a more target-like accent in the L2. After several years, she was passing as an NS of German not only due to her native-like accent as well as her clothing and manner, in order to be perceived as belonging to the L2 culture.

Passing not only involves use of the L2 but also avoidance of the L1, as Marx (2002) shows and as research by Moyer (2004), on L2 speakers of German, also illustrates. Moyer found that some of her participants at times actively avoided using certain L1 features, instead using L2 features to pass as an NS. Confidence in using the L2 was a major element in their L2 success. The more of the L2 they acquired, the more confidence they felt using the L2, and consequently, in developing a viable L2 identity. Moyer found that 'some participants describe how they "play" with language identity, i.e., purposefully misrepresenting their national heritage for their own amusement, as they put it' (p. 112). As she further states, 'The fact that these stories were not unusual shows that identity represents a conscious choice, that it is flexible and that there may be some special purpose in passing for a native speaker, particularly as a temporary performance' (pp. 112–113).

Identity related to ethnic group membership has also been examined, with much of the research focusing on EGA, defined as an individual's sense of belonging to a particular ethnic group. This work, led by Gatbonton and Trofimovich and colleagues, has primarily focused on Francophones and

Anglophones in Canada. Gatbonton and Trofimovich (2008) examined the relationship between English L2 proficiency and EGA, with proficiency assessed through English NS ratings on measures such as fluency, accentedness, and comprehensibility. For EGA, the researchers examined four dimensions, including group identification strength, group loyalty, views on language as expressing group identity, and group views on socio-political issues. The researchers found a significant association between EGA and L2 proficiency. Not all dimensions of EGA were significant, however. While group loyalty had no association with L2 proficiency, those with a higher EGA in the dimensions of language expressing group identity and group views on social-political issues had lower L2 proficiency ratings and tended to avoid using the L2. Gatbonton, Trofimovich, and Magid (2005) have found that Anglophone and Francophone L2 learners in Quebec ascribe EGA to their peers based on their L2 accents, indicating that L2 learners are aware of and participate in the assignment of social characteristics based on linguistic features.

Gatbonton, Trofimovich, and Segalowitz (2011) examined the correlation between EGA and the realization of the English voiced TH /ð/ as [d] (*th̲at* as *d̲at*), a typical pronunciation for French speakers of English as dental fricatives do not exist in French. They found that those with a higher Anglophone EGA had a greater use of the English [ð] versus those with a stronger Francophone EGA, who had a higher rate of realization of the voiced TH as the French [d]. The researchers found that greater support for the socio-political views or aspirations of their ethnic group was correlated with a less accurate L2 pronunciation overall.

The socio-political context may shape learners' viewpoints towards the L1 and L2 communities as well as L2 pronunciation attainment, as a range of studies by Gatbonton and Trofimovich and colleagues have shown. Gatbonton, Trofimovich, and Magid (2005) and Gatbonton and Trofimovich (2008) found that among Francophone learners of English L2, those who favoured independence for Quebec, a French-speaking providence in Canada, had a stronger L2 accent (more French-accented English). Similarly, Trofimovich, Turuševa, and Gatbonton (2013) reported that Latvian L1 learners of English with a stronger ethnic identification and stronger political views had lower self-ratings of their L2 ability.

As the research illustrates, acculturation into or identification with the L2 community may lead to greater L2 pronunciation attainment. This may be due to learners' 'accent aims' (Rindal, 2010) and investment in the development of a viable L2 identity through pronunciation attainment. For these learners, the development of a viable L2 identity through the use of salient features of the L2 may not be viewed as a threat to their L1 identity. The studies also highlight the creativity and ability of learners in using features of the L1 and L2 to pass as speakers of the L2 or retain their L1 ethnic or cultural identity while using the L2. The latter will now be discussed in more detail.

- *Learners may resist usage of some L2 features in order to retain an L1 identity.*

As noted previously, learners do not only acquire features of the L2, but they acquire sociolinguistic knowledge about the social meaning of different L2 features while acquiring the L2. As a result, they may target particular features to mark belonging or membership in a given social group as learners' accent aims (Rindal, 2010) translate into specific linguistic choices (see Sections 3 and 6). Similarly, as research by Ohara (2001) and Siegal (1996) (see Section 6) has shown, learners may avoid or resist usage of certain features of the L2 if they do not wish to project a viable L2 identity when they feel this is at odds with their L1 identity.

Research has found that a stronger identification with the L1 community is associated with a stronger foreign accent in the L2 through the retention of features of the L1 when using the L2. Sharma (2005), for example, found that the participants who had the lowest rates of usage of the variants associated with AmE were more aware and protective of their IndE identities. In research on ethnic identity in Canada, Gatbonton (1975) found that the use of English interdental fricatives was correlated with the learners' ethnic identity and that some learners with a young AOA used L1 features for social marking if they had strong connections to their L1 community and extensive use of the L1. Polat and Schallert (2013) found that the Kurdish participants who had stronger identification with the L1 community had a stronger foreign accent in the L2 than those who identified with the L2 community or both the L1 and L2 community. Lybeck (2002) found that the American women who had lower levels of acculturation into and identification with the Norwegian L2 community had higher rates of usage of the AmE realization of /r/ in contrast to higher rates of usage of the Norwegian /r/ among women who had higher levels of acculturation and identification with the Norwegian L2 community. Achirri (2017), in a case study of a university student in the United States from China, found that, through her experiences in the United States, the learner became more aware of her Chinese identity and the connection between accent and identity. As a result, she focused less on attaining a native-like AmE accent, choosing to retain her L1 (Chinese) accent.

If learners are unable to acculturate to the L2 culture and/or feel that accommodating linguistically to the L2 culture is an erasure of their L1 identity, they may actively resist targeting a more native-like pronunciation in the L2, instead preferring to use L1 features. The use of the L1 features, as noted throughout the

Element, may be erroneously be viewed as a lack of acquisition of the L2 rather than the agency of the L2 learner in deciding how to sound in the L2, including sounding like an L1 speaker of the L2.

- *Pronunciation features – in contrast to other linguistic features such as syntactic features – may be more salient markers of a particular identity.*

Research suggests that 'acts of identity' (Le Page and Tabouret-Keller, 1985) may be more saliently marked by pronunciation features than by other features such as syntactic features. This could be, as Sharma (2005) suggests, because pronunciation divergences from the standard or target language model or norm may be viewed more positively than syntactic divergences, which may be viewed more negatively or as errors. In research on speakers of IndE in the United States, Sharma (2005) found that her participants were more likely to use phonological features – including rhoticity, aspiration, and velarization – to sound American rather than syntactic features. As she notes,

> This difference in Indian English speakers' use of certain syntactic and certain phonological variants may be interpreted in two ways. First, syntactic variants may be indicators, and thus below the level of consciousness, not exploited stylistically, and not commented upon. Second, syntactic divergence may be consciously recognized but evaluated more negatively by some speakers, and thus not as willingly employed in stylistic work. (Sharma, 2005, p. 217)

Another explanation for the use of phonetic and phonological features for social marking is that phonological variation may be more salient or noticeable to L2 learners than syntactic features in variation. In other words, L2 learners may be more aware of how phonological features in the L2 are used to signify identity and group memberships and less likely to be aware of syntactic differences. Rhoticity and aspiration (see also Section 2) may be more noticeable to L2 learners due to their frequency and acoustic salience, as Hansen Edwards (2016) and Rindal (2010) have also found.

- *The readiness and/or ability to adopt a secondary identity (a L2 identity not in conflict with L1 identity) may be correlated with higher L2 pronunciation attainment and may be more common in settings where learners do not see a conflict or relationship between identity and accent.*

Whether the learners are acquiring the L2 in a foreign or L2 setting may impact their ability to develop a viable L2 identity that is not in conflict with their L1 identity. This, in turn, may impact their use of L2 features. When the L2 is a foreign language, learners may not perceive that attaining a target-like accent is a threat to their L1 identity as they are fully immersed in the L1 context.

In contexts where the language is being learned as an L2, particularly for migrants or immigrants who have long-term stay intentions, attaining a higher level of L2 pronunciation proficiency may be perceived as a threat to their L1 identity. As Block (2007, p. 5) states, 'It is in the migrant context, more than other contexts, that one's identity and sense of self are put on the line.'

Research on English as a foreign language (EFL) learners in Pakistan (Zahoor & Kausar, 2018), Turkey (Pullen, 2011), and Greece (Georgountzou &Tsantila, 2017) has found that L2 pronunciation attainment was not associated as a threat to the students' L1 cultural identity and that loyalty to their L1 culture did not impact the students' interest in attaining a more native-like accent in the L2. This is likely because the learners were studying the L2 in the L1 context. Georgountzou and Tsantila (2017), for example, reported that while the learners were proud of their Greek identities, they disassociated this from wanting to speak with a more native-like accent in the L2. In contrast, when learners are immigrants to the L2 community or learning the L2 in the L2 community, some learners may perceive that a more target-like L2 pronunciation attainment conflicts with their L1 identity, as studies by Polat and Schallert (2013), Ohara (2001), and Lybeck (2002), among others, have shown.

While research on L2 learners in the United States has shown that the L2 learners disassociate having a native-like L2 accent with threats to their L1 identity (Levis, 2015; McCrocklin & Link, 2016), this could be due to the international student status of the participants, and thus short-term stay intentions, as they may return to their home countries after their sojourn in the United States.

- *Speakers may construct a 'new' L2 or ethnic identity through the use of unique linguistic features.*

As Nance and colleagues (2016) state, while most L2 research has focused on either Type 1 variation (learner errors in using the L2) or Type 2 variation (the L2 acquisition of the sociolinguistic variation patterns found for native speakers of the L2), another kind of variation can exist. As they argue, learners may not wish to sound like NSs – they may have different accent aims and identity formations unique to their own linguistic situations. Nance and colleagues term this Type 3 variation – the emergence of new features or variants. A number of studies provide evidence of this.

In their own research on word-final rhotic variation among adult L2 learners of Scottish Gaelic in Scotland, Nance and colleagues (2016), found that the L2 learners had very little consistency in terms of Type 2 variation – in acquiring the sociolinguistic variation patterns found in the L2. They compared the 'new' speakers of Scottish Gaelic (the L2 learners) with older and more traditional speakers of Scottish Gaelic and found that there was significant variation in rhotic production among the new speakers that could not be explained by L1 transfer or approximation of NS norms. Through interviews with the participants, the researchers found that some participants aimed for a 'new speaker' identity in Scottish Gaelic, one that did not target a traditional Gaelic model. This identity was constructed in part through the lack of a phonemic distinction between rhotic categories, a distinction that was found for traditional speakers of Gaelic, or zero or weak realization of the rhotic in coda position (traditional speakers of Gaelic would have a rhotic realization in codas).

In research on first- (Gen I) and second-generation (Gen II) Russian immigrants in Australia, Gnevesheva (2020) focused on the GOOSE vowel (fronted in Australian English, AusE) and the TRAP vowel (raised in AusE). Gnevesheva found that while Gen I Russians had a more retracted (less fronted) realization of GOOSE (more Russian-like) than NSs of AusE, Gen II speakers had more fronted realization similar to NSs of AusE (referred to as 'Anglos' in this study). In addition, Gnevesheva found evidence of unique variation patterns among the Gen II speakers, as they had style shifting patterns not found among the Anglos, with their own norms for variation. The researcher found different linguistic constraints on GOOSE-fronting among the three groups of speakers. For TRAP, the Gen I had a more Russian-like realization. The differences among Anglo and Gen II realizations for TRAP was not statistically significant, however. Overall, the Gen I speakers had more Russian influence on their vowel realizations while the Gen II speakers differed from both Anglo and Gen I speakers for the realization of GOOSE. As both style shifting patterns (more retracted GOOSE in interview and reading styles) and linguistic environment differences were found for the Gen II speakers, the researcher posits that the Gen II speakers were constructing a new ethnolect, or ethnic linguistic identity, as NS of English with a Russian background.

Van Hofwegen (2009) conducted research on the realizations of the lateral approximant /l/ in onsets for three generations of Mexicans in America. As Van Hofwegen states, word-initial /l/ (as in *led*) has various realizations in varieties of AmE, with a lighter /l/ realizations in Chicano English (ChiE), a Spanish-influenced variety of AmE, than in other varieties of English in the United States. Van Hofwegen found that Gen III speakers had a lighter /l/ than Gen I and II, and Gen II had a darker /l/ than Gen I or III, suggesting that, while Gen II speakers, NSs of English raised in the United States, have features associated with a more standard or general AmE, Gen III speakers use variants associated with Spanish, possibly to enact a 'new' ethnic identity. As Van Hofwegen notes, this pattern has been found among other ethnic groups in the United States as well as in New Zealand. As she states, 'In these other communities, as prevalence of native languages has fallen away as younger generations acquire and use English as an L1, sociolinguists have found that often the particularly striking phonological and syntactical features of those receding languages will show up robustly in the newer dialects of English' (p. 319).

The re-emergence of features from heritage languages in the language used by newer generations is illustrated by findings from research on the use of English features by Native American and Canadian First Nations communities. Newmark, Walker, and Stanford (2016) found that members of these communities constructed a shared Indigenous ethnic identity using pitch accent and intonation contours, and tonal differences. These included contour pitch-accent, high-falling, high-rising, and mid terminals, lengthened intonation-unit-final syllables, and syllable timing. One reason for this, as the authors note, is that many of the younger members of these communities do not speak the heritage languages, and therefore use of suprasegmental features in English has become an important mechanism to express an Indigenous ethnic identity. The authors further state that while there are distinctive English features in use in some regions and ethnic communities, members of these communities across a wider geographical area construct and perform a shared Indigenous identity using prosodic features.

In summary, the use of features associated with the heritage language by newer generations of immigrants helps them establish an ethnic identity, in this case in English, particularly if they are not speakers of the heritage language and wish to index their cultural and ethnic association.

Identity and EGA research indicate that a strong identification with the L2 culture or both the L1 and L2 culture is associated with L2 pronunciation gains. Identification with the L1 and the L2 culture are not mutually exclusive – learners may shift between identities, using L1 and L2 features to mark identities in different contexts and among different social groups. Learners may actively use L2 features to pass as an NS of the L2 and member of the L2 community; L2 learners may also engage in language play with their linguistic identifies, again underscoring the agency of learners in using L1/L2 features to construct viable identifies across social contexts and social/peer groups. Learners in target-language settings, in particular, may choose to retain L1 features in the L2 to construct an L2 as an NS of another language. This may be more prevalent in contexts where L2 learners perceive that aiming to speak like a native speaker of the target language conflicts with or erases their L1 cultural identity. In other words, they retain features of the L1 in order to retain a visible – in this case through their L2 accents – marker of L1 ethnic and/or cultural membership.

8 Implications and Future Directions

This Element has attempted to address several key questions:

- What do we mean by social factors?
- Which social factors have been investigated in research on L2 phonological acquisition and use?
- How and why do social factors affect L2 phonological acquisition (production and perception) and use?

As the synthesis of research presented in this Element illustrates, learners acquire not only the L2, but information about how the L2 is used in different social groups and social situations. While a great deal is known about how social factors impact L1 and L2 acquisition and use, particularly in the areas of phonetics and phonology, more research is needed on:

- Learners in multilingual and multidialectal contexts
- Learners from less well studied populations
- Speakers of less well studied languages and dialects
- Languages attitudes and the targeting and use of dialectal/varietal/ethnolectal features
- Long-term gains and attrition after SA and/or IM
- Perception (awareness) of L2 features, attitudes towards the use of these features, and the use of the features
- Awareness of sociolinguistic variation in the L2
- The impact of teachers' ideologies on accent aims and L2 use
- Differential gains on L2 features through IM, SA, and L2 contact and exposure
- The adoption of regional/dialectal variants by learners versus the lack of adoption by others
- The impact of the length of the SA on L2 pronunciation gains
- The impact of the SA experience and/or SNs on L2 accent aims and attitudes
- The development of 'new speaker' identities in the L2 (Type 3 variation)
- The development of intelligibility (in contrast to research focusing on 'degree of foreign accent' or segmental/suprasegmental L2 gains) during the SA or through L2 contact and exposure and SNs
- The impact of the context of the SA (France vs. China, for example) on L2 gains
- Age as a social construct – how the age of L2 learners impacts the learners' ability to develop and access meaningful L2 use opportunities leading to L2 gains.

A final question this Element seeks to answer is: *What are the implications of these findings for teaching L2 pronunciation?* Based on the findings outlined in the Element, the following suggestions are offered for teaching:

- Teachers should be aware of their own ideologies about the L2, its speakers, and its culture, and that their ideologies may directly impact learners' attitudes towards L2 features and dialects of the L2.
- Divergences from what is taught in the L2 classroom versus what the L2 speaker does in the L2 do not signify errors or lack of acquisition. Instead, the differences may illustrate the features the L2 learner is targeting based on their accent aims, L2 peer and social groups, and L1/L2 identity.
- Exposure to mass media outside the classroom influences what learners target for acquisition and use and may be more impactful on accent aims than the models taught in the language classroom.
- L2 pronunciation assessments constructed based on classroom models may inadvertently underestimate or provide a limited view of the L2 learners' actual knowledge about and ability in the L2.
- L2 pronunciation gains are fostered not only through pronunciation-based activities. Engaging with the L2 across a range of modes – writing, speaking, listening, and reading – is associated with L2 pronunciation gains.
- Adult learners may have more difficulty than child learners in developing SNs through which they can be facilitated in L2 use.
- Differential outcomes in L2 pronunciation attainment by girls/women and boys/men are explainable by a range of factors including ideologies about girls/women as better language learners, increased access to educational and occupational opportunities through more standard language use and gendered L1/L2 cultural norms. Contrary to popular belief, however, there is no innate biological advantage for girls/women in language learning over boys/men.
- Gender plays a role in giving learners access to different social groups in the L2 culture, and this impacts the L2 pronunciation features targeted by girls/women versus boys/men.

The following suggestions are offered for teachers:

- Hold classroom discussions about the different dialects of the L2, and how phonetic/phonological features differ across varieties of the L2. As an example, teachers can discuss the use of DH-stopping, the realization of the voiced TH /ð/ as [d], across different varieties of English, to increase learners' awareness of how speech sounds vary across dialects of the L2.
- Incorporate sociolinguistic variation patterns into L2 teaching, to help learners achieve socio-phonetic and socio-phonological competence. This is

particularly important if the L2 is taught as a second language or if learners are intending to go on an SA in the L2 culture. Learners of L2 French, as an example, would benefit from instruction on schwa and /l / deletion patterns in French, to aid L2 productive and perceptive knowledge.

- Provide explicit L2 pronunciation instruction to learners before an SA experience, particularly with regards to the features relevant to dialect(s) spoken in the SA contexts. For learners of L2 Spanish in the United States going on an SA in Spain, for example, explicit instruction on the realization of /s/ variably as [s] or [θ] in some dialects of Spanish would support their L2 gains during the SA and increase their L2 perceptual and productive abilities during the SA.
- Develop more flexible L2 pronunciation assessments that allow learners to demonstrate a wider range of L2 productive and perceptual abilities in the L2 beyond the models taught in class. Local or dialectal features of the L2 can be incorporated into assessments, to represent a wide range of linguistic choices available to learners in a given L2 context. If the focus of assessment is gains in vowel accuracy, as an example, variation in vowel realizations such as the fronting of GOOSE and FOOT should be incorporated into the assessments (if they are in use among target-language speakers in the local community).
- Engage students in creating more interesting and relevant teaching materials through a discussion of students' accent aims and preferences rather than presupposing that learners are targeting a particular language model or norm. Learners can conduct small research projects on features of the L2 that they are aware of, such as T Glottaling, DH-stopping, aspiration versus flapping, and rhoticity in English. Students and the teacher can then engage in an examination of the social meaning of these variables across different dialects of English and develop sociolinguistically appropriate dialogues for L2 practice that incorporate these features. As an example, a dialogue between a speaker of AmE and BrE can be developed incorporating words with postvocalic /r/ such as *car* (Speaker A: *Where did the driver park the car?* Speaker B: *I heard the car enter the car park*) to showcase the differences in rhoticity between these two varieties of English.
- Incorporate a range of L2 activities in the classroom, including reading, writing, listening, and speaking, and encourage learners to engage with the L2 in various modes outside the classroom. Learners should be encouraged to not only speak the L2 to make L2 pronunciation gains, but they should read and write in the L2 and spend time listening to a range of speakers of the L2 (see Table 7 for resources).
- Establish language-exchange or language practice opportunities for adult learners with target-language speakers, to help adult learners to develop

Table 7 Online databases

Website name	Languages/ Varieties	Link
The Audio Archive	English	http://www.alt-usage-english.org/audio_archive.html
English Accents Worldwide	English	https://www.eng.cuhk.edu.hk/ENGE-EAWW/
Speech Accent Archive	English	https://accent.gmu.edu/
International Dialects of English Archive (IDEA)	English	https://www.dialectsarchive.com/globalmap
The History and Spread of English Worldwide	English	https://www.eng.cuhk.edu.hk/ENGE-MAP/
VADA: Visual Accent and Dialect Archive	English	https://visualaccentdialectarchive.com/
University College London (UCL) Speaker Database	English	https://www.phon.ucl.ac.uk/shop/uclspeaker.php
British National Corpus	English	https://sounds.bl.uk/Accents-and-dialect
The IViE Corpus: English Intonation in the British Isles	English	http://www.phon.ox.ac.uk/files/apps/IViE/
Santa Barbara Corpus of Spoken American English	English	https://www.linguistics.ucsb.edu/research/
Wellington Corpus of Spoken New Zealand English	English	http://korpus.uib.no/icame/manuals/WSC/INDEX.HTM

Table 7 (cont.)

Website name	**Languages/ Varieties**	**Link**
Sound Comparisons	German Spanish English French Celtic languages	https://soundcomparisons.com/#home
Telling Stories	Chinese English French German Dutch Irish Portuguese Scots Scottish Gaelic Indonesian Hindi Bangla/Bengali Japanese Korean	https://www.eng.cuhk.edu.hk/ENGE-TellingStories/index.html

	Nepali	
	Tagalog	
	Urdu	
	Vietnamese	
	Afrikaans	
	Amharic	
	Igbo	
	Lugandan	
	Oromo	
	Shona	
	Kiswahili	
The Linguistics of Spanish	Spanish	https://www.staff.ncl.ac.uk/i.e.mackenzie/index.html
History and Dialectology of Spanish	Spanish	https://people.cas.sc.edu/deholt01/links/Historyofspanishlinks .html#Valencian
Eurolinguiste	French	http://eurolinguiste.com/look-languages-dialects-france/
Voices.com	French	https://www.voices.com/blog/types-of-french/
Phonemica	Chinese	https://phonemica.net/
YouGlish	English	https://youglish.com/
	Thai German	https://youglish.com/thai
	Korean	https://youglish.com/german
	Italian	https://youglish.com/korean
	Arabic	https://youglish.com/italian
	Japanese	https://youglish.com/arabic
		https://youglish.com/japanese

viable SNs and opportunities for L2 use. This may be particularly important for adult immigrants to the target-language culture as they may not be able to develop SNs on their own outside the language classroom.

- Integrate online media, including YouTube, online databases, and music, films, and TV shows, into classroom materials to expose learners to the L2 and to variation in the L2 across speakers and contexts. A list of online databases to support language teaching is given in Table 7.

Appendix

Table 8 Keywords in Wells' (1982) lexical sets

Keyword	RP	GAmE	Example words
KIT	ɪ	ɪ	ship, sick, bridge, milk, myth, busy
DRESS	e	ɛ	step, neck, edge, shelf, friend, ready
TRAP	æ	æ	tap, back, badge, scalp, hand, cancel
LOT	ɒ	ɑ	stop, sock, dodge, romp, possible, quality
STRUT	ʌ	ʌ	cup, suck, budge, pulse, trunk, blood
FOOT	ʊ	ʊ	put, bush, full, good, look, wolf
BATH	ɑː	æ	staff, brass, ask, dance, sample, calf
CLOTH	ɒ	ɔ	cough, broth, cross, long, Boston
NURSE	ɜː	ɜr	hurt, lurk, urge, burst, jerk, term
FLEECE	iː	i	creep, speak, leave, feel, key, people
FACE	eɪ	eɪ	tape, cake, raid, veil, steak, day
PALM	ɑː	ɑ	psalm, father, bra, spa, lager
THOUGHT	ɔː	ɔ	taught, sauce, hawk, jaw, broad
GOAT	əʊ	o	soap, joke, home, know, so, roll
GOOSE	uː	u	loop, shoot, tomb, mute, huge, view
PRICE	aɪ	aɪ	ripe, write, arrive, high, try, buy
CHOICE	ɔɪ	ɔɪ	adroit, noise, join, toy, royal
MOUTH	aʊ	aʊ	out, house, loud, count, crowd, cow
NEAR	ɪə	ɪr	beer, sincere, fear, beard, serum
SQUARE	ɛə	ɛr	care, fair, pear, where, scarce, vary
START	ɑː	ɑr	far, sharp, bark, carve, farm, heart
NORTH	ɔː	ɔr	for, war, short, scorch, born, warm
FORCE	ɔː	or	four, wore, sport, porch, borne, story
CURE	ʊə	ʊr	poor, tourist, pure, plural, jury
*HAPP*Y	ɪ	ɪ	copy, scampi, taxi, sortie, committee, hockey, Chelsea
*LETT*ER	ə	ər	paper, metre, calendar, stupor, succo(u)r, martyr, figure
*COMM*A	ə	ə	catalpa, quota, vodka

(Wells 1982, vol. 2, pp. xviii–xix)

List of Abbreviations

AAVE	African American Vernacular English
AH	At home
AmE	American English
AOA	Age of Arrival
AusE	Australian English
BrE	British English
ChiE	Chicano English
EFL	English as a foreign language
EGA	Ethnic group affiliation
ESL	English as a second language
FI	Formal instruction
GAmE	General American English
IM	Immersion
IndE	Indian English
IrE	Irish English
L1	First language
L2	Second language
LOR	Length of residence
MGT	Matched guise test
MLE	Multicultural London English
NS	Native speaker
RP	Received pronunciation
SA	Study abroad
SgE	Singapore English
SN	Social network
SSBE	Standard Southern British English
VGT	Verbal guise test
VOT	Voice onset time

Bibliography

Key Readings

The following readings are recommended to further the understanding of social factors and L2 phonetics and phonology. These are referenced in the Element.

Hansen Edwards, J. G. (2008). Social factors and variation in production in L2 phonology. In J. G. Hansen Edwards & M. L. Zampini (Eds.). *Phonology and Second Language Acquisition*. Amsterdam: John Benjamins, pp. 251–79.

Moyer, A. (2004). *Age, accent and experience in second language acquisition* Amsterdam Mouton de Gruyter.

Nance, C. McLeod, W., O'Rourke, B. , & Dunmore, S. (2016). Identity, accent aim, and motivation in second language users: New Scottish Gaelic speakers' use of phonetic variation. *Journal of Sociolinguistics 20*(2), 164–91.

Piske T., Mackay, I. R. A., & Flege, J. E. (2001). Factors affecting degree of foreign accent in an L2: a review. *Journal of Phonetics 29*(2), 191–215.

Rindal, U. (2010). Constructing identity with L2: Pronunciation and attitudes among Norwegian learners of English. *Journal of Sociolinguistics 14*(2), 240–61.

Schoonmaker-Gates, E. (2020). The acquisition of dialect-specific phonology, phonetics, and sociolinguistics in L2 spanish. *Critical Multilingualism Studies 8*(1), 80–103.

References

Achirri, K. (2017). Perceiving identity through accent lenses: A case study of a Chinese English speaker's perceptions of her pronunciation and perceived social identity. *MSU Working Papers in SLS 8*, 5–19.

Adamson, H., & Regan, V. (1991). The acquisition of community speech norms by Asian immigrants learning English as a second language: A preliminary study. *Studies in Second Language Acquisition 13*(1), 1–22.

Ader, K., & Miljan, M. (2015). External factors and the interference of L1 Estonian on L2 English pronunciation: An apparent-time study. *Estonian Papers in Applied Linguistics 11*, 21–35.

Alfayez, H. M., & Hüttner, J. (2019). Women students from Saudi Arabia in a study abroad programme. *Study Abroad Research in Second Language Acquisition and International Education 4*(2), 193–223.

Alvord, S. M., & Christiansen, D. E. (2012). Factors influencing the acquisition of Spanish voiced stop spirantization during an extended stay abroad. *Studies in Hispanic and Lusophone Linguistics 5*(2), 239–76.

Anisman, P. H. (1975). Some aspects of code switching in New York-Puerto Rican English. *Bilingual Review 2*, 56–85.

Avello, P., & Lara, A. R. (2014). Phonological development in L2 speech production during study abroad programmes differing in length of stay. In C. Perez-Vidal (Ed.), *Language acquisition in study abroad and formal instruction contexts*. Philadelphia, PA: John Benjamins, pp. 137–66.

Avello, P., Mora, J. C., & Pérez-Vidal, C. (2012). Perception of FA by non-native listeners in a study abroad context. *Research in Language 10*(1), 63–78.

Baker-Smemoe, W., Dewey, D. P., Bown, J., & Martinsen, R. A. (2014). Variables affecting L2 gains during study abroad. *Foreign Language Annals 47*(3), 464–86.

Baten, K. (2020). The role of social networks and intense friendships in study abroad students' L2 use and speaking development. *Study Abroad Research in Second Language Acquisition and International Education 5*(1), 15–44.

Bejarano, M., Dewey, D. P., Baker-Smemoe, W., Henrichsen, L. E., & Hall, T. (2019). Adult second language learners' social network development and perceived fluency gains in an intensive English program abroad. *Study Abroad Research in Second Language Acquisition and International Education 4*(2), 168–92.

Bielby, D. D., & Harrington, C. L. (2008). *Global TV: Exporting television and culture in the world market*. New York: New York University Press.

Block, D. (2007). *Second language identities*. London: Continuum.

Cameron, D. (2005). Language, gender, and sexuality: Current issues and new directions. *Applied Linguistics 26*(4), 482–502.

Casillas, J. V. (2020). The longitudinal development of fine-phonetic detail: Stop production in a domestic immersion programme. *Language Learning 70* (3), 768–806.

Chan, J. Y. H. (2018). Gender and attitudes towards English varieties: Implications for teaching English as a global language. *System 76*, 62–79.

Chappell, W., & Kanwit, M. (2022). Do learners connect sociophonetic variation with regional and social characteristics? The case of L2 perception of Spanish aspiration. *Studies in Second Language Acquisition 44*(1), 185–209.

Cheshire, J., Kerswill, P., Fox, S., & Torgersen, E. (2011). Contact, the feature pool and the speech community: The emergence of Multicultural London English. *Journal of Sociolinguistics 15*(2), 151–96.

Clark, L., & Schleef, E. (2010). The acquisition of sociolinguistic evaluations among Polish-born adolescents learning English: Evidence from perception. *Language Awareness 19*(4), 299–322.

Clark, U. (2007). *Studying language: English in action*. Basingstoke: Palgrave Macmillan.

Coates, J., & Pichler, P. (2011). *Language and gender: A reader*. 2nd ed. Hoboken, NJ: Wiley-Blackwell.

Derwing, T. M., Munro, M. J., & Thomson, R. I. (2007). A longitudinal study of ESL learners' fluency and comprehensibility development. *Applied Linguistics 29*(3), 359–80.

Díaz-Campos, M. (2004). Context of learning in the acquisition of Spanish second language phonology. *Studies in Second Language Acquisition 26*(2), 249–73.

Díaz-Campos, M. (2006). The effect of style in second language phonology: An analysis of segmental acquisition in study abroad and regular-classroom students. In C. A. Klee and T. L. Face (Eds.), *Selected proceedings of the 7th Conference on the Acquisition of Spanish and Portuguese as First and Second Languages*. Somerville, MA: Cascadilla Proceedings Project, pp. 26–39.

Diskin, C., & Levey, S. (2019). Going global and sounding local: Quotative variation and change in L1 and L2 speakers of Irish (Dublin) English. *English World-Wide 40*(1), 53–78.

Dollman, J., Kogan, I., & Weißmann, M. (2020). Speaking accent-free in L2 beyond the critical period: The compensatory role of individual abilities and opportunity structures. *Applied Linguistics 41*(5), 787–809.

Drummond, R. (2010). *Sociolinguistic variation in a second language: The influence of local accent on the pronunciation of non-native English speakers living in Manchester*. Unpublished doctoral dissertation, Manchester Metropolitan University.

Drummond, R. (2011). Glottal variation in /t/ in non-native English speech. *English World Wide 32*(3), 280–308.

Eckert, P., & McConnell-Ginet, S. (1999). New generalizations and explanations in language and gender research. *Language in Society 28*, 185–201.

Ehrlich, S. (1997). Gender as social practice: Implications for second language acquisition. *Studies in Second Language Acquisition 19*(4), 421–46.

Freed, B. F., Segalowitz, N., & Dewey, D. (2004). Context of learning and second language fluency in French: Comparing regular classroom, study abroad and intensive domestic immersion programs. *Studies in Second Language Acquisition 26*, 275–301.

Gardner, R. (1985). *Social psychology and second language learning: The role of attitudes and motivation*. London: Edward Arnold.

Garrett, P. (2007). Language attitudes. In C. Llamas, L. Mullany, & P. Stockwell (Eds.), *The Routledge companion to sociolinguistics*. New York: Routledge, pp. 116–21.

Gatbonton, E. (1975). Systematic variations in second language speech: A sociolinguistic study. Unpublished PhD dissertation, McGill University, Montreal, Canada.

Gatbonton, E., Trofimovich, P., & Magid, M. (2005). Learners' ethnic group affiliation and L2 pronunciation accuracy: A sociolinguistic investigation. *TESOL Quarterly 39*(3), 489–511.

Gatbonton, E., & Trofimovich, P. (2008). The ethnic group affiliation and L2 proficiency link: Empirical evidence. *Language Awareness 17*(3), 229–48.

Gatbonton, E., Trofimovich, P., & Segalowitz, N. (2011). Ethnic group affiliation and patterns of development of a phonological variable. *The Modern Language Journal 95*(ii), 188–204.

Georgountzou, A., & Tsantila, N. (2017). Cultural identity, accentedness and attitudes of Greek EFL learners towards English pronunciation. In E. Agathopoulou, T. Danavassi, & L. Efststhiadi (Eds.), *Selected papers on the 22nd International Symposium on Theoretical and Applied Linguistics*. Thessaloniki: Aristotle University of Thessaloniki Press, pp. 160–74.

Gluszek, A., Newheiser, A.-K., & Dovidio, J. F. (2011). Social psychological orientations and accent strength. *Journal of Language and Social Psychology 30*(1), 28–45.

Gnevesheva, K. (2020). The role of style in the ethnolect: Style-shifting in the use of ethnolectal features in first-and second-generation speakers. *International Journal of Bilingualism 24*(4), 861–80.

Grammon, D. (2021). Consequential choices: A language ideological perspective on learners' (non-)adoption of a dialectal variant. *Foreign Language Annals 54*, 607–25.

Habib, R. (2014). Vowel variation and reverse acquisition in rural Syrian child and adolescent language. *Language Variation and Change 26*, 45–75.

Hansen Edwards, J. G. (2008). Social factors and variation in production in L2 phonology. In J. G. Hansen Edwards & M. L. Zampini (Eds.), *Phonology and second language acquisition*. Amsterdam: John Benjamins, pp. 251–79.

Hansen Edwards, J. G. (2009). *Acquiring a non-native phonology: Linguistic constraints and social barriers*. London: Continuum.

Hansen Edwards, J. G. (2016). Accent preferences and the use of American English features in Hong Kong: A preliminary study. *Asian Englishes 18*(3), 197–215.

Hansen Edwards, J. G., Chan, R., Lam, T., & Wang, Q. (2021). Social factors and the teaching of pronunciation: What the research tells us. In

M. Pennington (Ed.), Teaching Pronunciation, special issue *RELC Journal 52*(1), 35–47.

Henriksen, N. C., Geeslin, K. L., & Willis, E. W. (2010). The development of L2 Spanish intonation during a study abroad immersion program in Leon, Spain: Global contours and final boundary movements. *Studies in Hispanic and Lusophone Linguistics 3*(1), 113–62.

Hiang, T. C., & Gupta, A. F. (1992). Post-vocalic /r/ in Singapore English. In S. J. Harlow, & A. R. Warner (Eds.), *York Papers in Linguistics 16*, 139–52.

Howley, G. (2015). The acquisition of Manchester dialect variants by adolescent Roma migrants. Unpublished PhD dissertation, School of Arts and Media, University of Salford, UK.

Huensch, A., Tracy-Ventura, N., Bridges, J., & Cuesta Medina, J. A. (2019). Variables affecting the maintenance of L2 proficiency and fluency four years post-study abroad. *Study Abroad Research in Second Language Acquisition and International Education 4*(1), 96–125.

Højen, A. (2003). Second-language speech perception and production in adult learners before and after short-term immersion. PhD dissertation, Aarhus University, Aarhus, Denmark.

Jenkins, J. (2000) *The phonology of English as an international language: new models, new norms, new goals*. Oxford: Oxford University Press.

Kennedy Terry, K. M. (2017). Contact, context, and collocation: The emergence of sociostylistic variation in L2 French learners during study abroad. *Studies in Second Language Acquisition 39*, 553–78.

Kennedy Terry, K. M. (2022). At the intersection of SLA and sociolinguistics: The predictive power of social networks during study abroad. *The Modern Language Journal 106*(1), 245–66.

Kissling, E. (2014). What predicts the effectiveness of foreign-language pronunciation instruction? Investigating the role of perception and other individual differences. *Canadian Modern Language Review/La Revue canadienne des langues vivantes*, *70*(4), 532–58.

Kroskrity, P. V. (2016). Language ideologies and language attitudes. Oxford Bibliographies. 28 April. www.oxfordbibliographies.com/view/document/obo- 9780199772810/obo-9780199772810–0122.xml.

Kwek, G., & Low, E.-L. (2021). Emergent features of young Singaporean speech: An investigatory study of the labiodental /r/ in Singapore English. *Asian Englishes 23*(2), 116–36.

Labov, W. (1990). The intersection of sex and social class in the course of linguistic change. *Language Variation and Change 2*(2), 205–54.

Lambert, W. E. (1967). A social psychology of bilingualism. *Journal of Social Issues 23*(2), 91–109.

Lambert, W. E., Frankel, H., & Tucker, G. R. (1966). Judging personality through speech: A French-Canadian example. *Journal of Communication 16*, 305–21.

Le Page, R., & Tabouret-Keller, A. (1985). *Acts of identity: Creole-based approaches to language and ethnicity.* Cambridge: Cambridge University Press.

Levis, J. M. (2015). Learners' views of social issues in pronunciation learning. *Journal of Academic Language & Learning* 9(1), 42–55.

Llanes, A. (2016). The influence of a short stay abroad experience on perceived foreign accent: An exploratory study beyond the immediate effects. *Study Abroad Research in Second Language Acquisition and International Education 1*(1), 88–106.

Lord, G. (2010). The combined effects of immersion and instruction on second language pronunciation. *Foreign Language Annals 43*(3), 488–503.

Lybeck, K. (2002). Cultural identification and second language pronunciation of Americans in Norway. *The Modern Language Journal 86*(2), 174–91.

Martinson, R. A. (2008). Short-term study abroad: Predicting changes in oral skills. *Foreign Language Annals 43*(3), 504–30.

Martinsen, R. A., Alvord, S. M., & Tanner, J. (2014). Perceived foreign accent: Extended stays abroad, level of instruction, and motivation. *Foreign Language Annals 47*(1), 66–78.

Marx, N. 2002. Never quite a 'native speaker': Accent and identity in the L2 – and the L1. *The Canadian Modern Language Review/La Revue Canadienne des Langues Vivantes* 59, 264–81.

McCrocklin, S. and Link, S. (2016). Accent, identity, and a fear of loss? ESL students' perspectives. *The Canadian Modern Language Review 72*(1), 122–48.

Meyerhoff, M., & Schleef, E. (2012). Variation, contact and social indexicality in the acquisition of (ing) by teenage migrants. *Journal of Sociolinguistics 16* (3), 398–416.

Milroy, J., & Milroy, L. (1985). Linguistic change, social network and speaker innovation. *Journal of Linguistics 21*, 339–84.

Milroy, L., & Milroy, J. (1992). Social network and social class: Towards an integrated sociolinguistic model. *Language in Society 21*, 1–26.

Mora, J. C. (2008). Learning context effects on the acquisition of a second language phonology. In C. Perez-Vidal, M. Juan-Garau, & A. Bel (Eds.), *A portrait of the young in the new multilingual Spain.* Clevendon: Multilingual Matters, 241–63.

Mora, J. C., & Valls-Ferrer, M. (2012). Oral fluency, accuracy, and complexity in formal instruction and study abroad learning contexts. *TESOL Quarterly 46*(4), 610–41.

Moyer, A. (2004). *Age, accent and experience in second language acquisition.* Amsterdam Mouton de Gruyter.

Moyer, A. (2007). Do language attitudes determine accent? A study of bilinguals in the USA. *Journal of Multilingual and Multicultural Development 28* (6), 502–18.

Moyer, A. (2011). An investigation of experience in L2 phonology: Does quality matter more than quantity? *The Canadian Modern Language Review/La Revue canadienne des langues vivantes*, *67*(2), 191–216.

Moyer, A. (2016). The puzzle of gender effects in L2 phonology. *Journal of Second Language Pronunciation*, *2*(1), 8–28.

Müller, M. (2016). Listening to learners' voices. *Journal of Second Language Pronunciation 2*(1), 108–42.

Munoz, C., & Llanes, A. (2014). Study abroad and changes in degree of foreign accent in children and adults. *Modern Language Journal 98*(1), 432–49.

Nagle, C., Morales-Front, A., Moorman, C., & Sanz, C. (2016). Disentangling research on study abroad and pronunciation. In D. M. Velliaris & D. Coleman-George D (Eds.), *Handbook of research on study abroad programs and outbound mobility.* Hershey, PA: IGI Global, 673–95.

Nance, C. (2020). Bilingual language exposure and the peer group: Acquiring phonetics and phonology in Gaelic Medium Education. *International Journal of Bilingualism*, *24*(2), 360–75.

Nance, C. McLeod, W., O'Rourke, B., & Dunmore, S. (2016). Identity, accent aim, and motivation in second language users: New Scottish Gaelic speakers' use of phonetic variation. *Journal of Sociolinguistics*, *20*(2), 164–91.

Newmark, K., Walker, N. and Stanford, J. (2016). 'The rez accent knows no borders': Native American ethnic identity expressed through English prosody. *Language in Society*, *45*, 633–64.

Ohara, Y. (2001). Finding one's voice in Japanese: a study of the pitch levels of L2 users. In A. Pavlenko, A. Blackledge, I. Piller, & M. Teutsch-Dwyer (Eds.), *Multilingualism, Second Language Learning and Gender.* Berlin: De Gruyter Mouton, 231–54.

Piske T., Mackay, I. R. A., and Flege, J. E. (2001). Factors affecting degree of foreign accent in an L2: A review. *Journal of Phonetics*, *29*(2), 191–215.

Poedjosoedarmo, G. (2000). The media as a model and source of innovation in the development of Singapore Standard English. In D. D. A. Brown & L. E. Ling (Eds.), *The English language in Singapore: Research on pronunciation*. Singapore: Singapore Association for Applied Linguistics, 112–20.

Polat, N., & Mahalingappa, L. J. (2010). Gender differences in identity and acculturation patterns and L2 accent attainment. *Journal of Language, Identity, and Education*, *9*(1), 17–35.

Polat, N., & Schallert, D. (2013). Kurdish adolescents acquiring Turkish: Their self-determined motivation and identification with L1 and L2 communities as predictors of L2 accent attainment. *The Modern Language Journal*, *97*(3), 745–63.

Pullen, E. (2011). Cultural identity, pronunciation, and attitudes of Turkish speakers of English: language identity in an EFL context. In J. Levis & K. Le Velle K (Eds.), *Proceedings of the 3rd Pronunciation in Second Language Learning and Teaching Conference*. Ames: Iowa State University, 65–83.

Purcell, E. T., & Suter, R. W. (1980). Predictors of pronunciation accuracy: A reexamination. *Language Learning*, *30*(2), 271–87.

Rindal, U. (2010). Constructing identity with L2: Pronunciation and attitudes among Norwegian learners of English. *Journal of Sociolinguistics*, *14*(2), 240–61.

Rindal, U., & Piercy, C. (2013). Being 'neutral'? English pronunciation among Norwegian learners. *World Englishes*, *32*(2), 211–29.

Ringer-Hilfinger, K. (2012) Learner acquisition of dialect variation in a study abroad context: the case of the Spanish [θ]. *Foreign Language Annals*, *45*(3), 1–17.

Schmidt, L. B. (2020). Role of developing language attitudes in a study abroad context on adoption of dialectal pronunciations. *Foreign Language Annals*, *53*(4), 785–806.

Schleef, E., Meyerhoff, M., & Clark, L. (2011) Teenagers' acquisition of variation: A comparison of locally-born and migrant teens' realisation of English (ing) in Edinburgh and London. *English World-Wide: A Journal of Varieties of English*, *32*(2), 206–36.

Segalowitz, N., Freed, B., Collentine, J., Lafford, B., Lazar, N., & Díaz-Campos, N. (2004). A comparison of Spanish second language acquisition in two different learning contexts: Study abroad and the domestic classroom. F*rontiers: The Interdisciplinary Journal of Study Abroad* *10*(1), 1–18.

Sharma, D. (2005). Dialect stabilization and speaker awareness in non-native dialects of English. *Journal of Sociolinguistics*, *9*(2), 194–224.

Sharma, D. (2011). Style repertoire and social change in British Asian English. *Journal of Sociolinguistics*, *15*(4), 464–92.

Shively, R. L. (2008). L2 Acquisition of [β], [ð], and [ɣ] in Spanish: impact of experience, linguistic environment, and learner variables. *Southwest Journal of Linguistics*, *27*(2), 79–114.

Siegal, M. (1996). The role of learner subjectivity in second language sociolinguistic competency: Western women learning Japanese. *Applied Linguistics*, *17*(3), 356–82.

Solon, M., & Kanwit, M. (2022). New methods for tracking development of sociophonetic competence: Exploring a preference task for Spanish /d/ deletion. *Applied Linguistics*, *43*(4), 805–25.

Stevens, J. J. (2011). Vowel duration in second language Spanish vowels: Study abroad versus at home learners. *Arizona Working Papers in SLA & Teaching*, *18*, 77–104.

Suter, R. W. (1976). Predictors of pronunciation accuracy in second language learning. *Language Learning*, *26*(1), 233–53.

Tan, Y.-Y. (2012). To *r* or not to *r*: Social correlates of /ɹ/ in Singapore English. *International Journal of the Sociology of Language*, *218*, 1–24.

Thompson, I. (1991). Foreign accents revisited: The English pronunciation of Russian immigrants. *Language Learning*, *41*(1), 177–204.

Trenchs-Parera, M. (2009). Effects of formal instruction and a stay abroad on the acquisition of native-like oral fluency. *Canadian Modern Language Review*, *65*(3), 365–93.

Trimble, J. (2013). Acquiring variable L2 Spanish intonation in a study abroad context. Unpublished PhD thesis, University of Minnesota.

Trofimovich, P., & Baker, W. (2006). Learning second language suprasegmentals: Effect of L2 experience on prosody and fluency characteristics of L2 speech. *Studies in Second Language Acquisition*, *28*(1), 1–30.

Trofimovich, P., Turuševa, L., & Gatbonton, E. (2013). Group membership and identity issues in second language learning. *Language Teaching 46*(4), 563–7.

Trudgill, P. (2001). *Sociolinguistics: An introduction to language and society.* 4th ed. New York: Penguin Random House.

Van Hofwegen, J. (2009). Cross-generational change in /l/ in Chicano English. *English World-Wide*, *30*(3), 302–25.

Wells, J. C. (1982). *Accents of English. Volumes I and 2.* Cambridge: Cambridge University Press.

Woolard, K. A. (2020). Language ideology. In J. Stanlaw (Ed.), *The International Encyclopedia of Linguistic Anthropology.* Hoboken, NJ: Wiley, 1–21.

Zahoor, M. & Kausar, G. (2018) Learning native-like English pronunciation and cultural identity. *New Horizons*, *12*(2), 19–32.

Cambridge Elements ☰

Phonetics

David Deterding

Universiti Brunei Darussalam

David Deterding is a Professor at Universiti Brunei Darussalam. His research has involved the measurement of rhythm, description of the pronunciation of English in Singapore, Brunei, and China, and the phonetics of Austronesian languages such as Malay, Brunei Malay, and Dusun.

Advisory Board

About the Series

The Cambridge Elements in Phonetics series will generate a range of high-quality scholarly works, offering researchers and students authoritative accounts of current knowledge and research in the various fields of phonetics. In addition, the series will provide detailed descriptions of research into the pronunciation of a range of languages and language varieties. There will be elements describing the phonetics of the major languages of the world, such as French, German, Chinese, and Malay as well as the pronunciation of endangered languages, thus providing a valuable resource for documenting and preserving them.

Cambridge Elements Ξ

Phonetics

Elements in the series

The Phonetics of Malay
David Deterding, Ishamina Athirah Gardiner and Najib Noorashid

Phonetics in Language Teaching
Di Liu, Tamara Jones and Marnie Reed

Spontaneous Speech
Benjamin V. Tucker and Yoichi Mukai

Phonetics and Phonology in Multilingual Language Development
Ulrike Gut, Romana Kopečková and Christina Nelson

Social Factors and L2 Phonetics and Phonology
Jette G. Hansen Edwards

A full series listing is available at: www.cambridge.org/EIPH

For EU product safety concerns, contact us at Calle de José Abascal, 56–1°,
28003 Madrid, Spain or eugpsr@cambridge.org.

www.ingramcontent.com/pod-product-compliance
Ingram Content Group UK Ltd.
Pitfield, Milton Keynes, MK11 3LW, UK
UKHW022146080726
473066UK00010B/790

* 9 7 8 1 1 0 8 9 3 2 0 2 8 *